the Pieces

LEISURE ARTS, INC.
Maumelle, Arkansas

Library of Congress Control Number: 2013948966

ISBN-13: 978-1-60900-676-1

6

18

30

36

42

54

66

72

Table of Contents

MEET THE DESIGNER
Lorna Miser

Lorna Miser is a knitting designer and the founder of Lorna's Laces, a popular line of hand-dyed yarns. A yarn industry celebrity, she travels the country teaching knitting and knitwear design.

"I was a seamstress when I was younger, which I'm sure helps me understand the fit of garments," Lorna says. "I like designs that are relaxing to knit, with just enough happening to keep your interest but simple enough to not have to read the pattern every row." Most of all, though, she says, "I just enjoy creating and playing with pretty yarns and colors!"

The author of *Faith, Hope, Love, Knitting* and *The Knitter's Guide to Hand-Dyed and Variegated Yarn*, Lorna lives in Folsom, California. "I live near the famous Folsom Prison (of Johnny Cash's song), where there are hundreds of miles of bike trails along the American River," she says. "I enjoy riding there or cruising through town in my purple '65 convertible Mustang."

12

24

48

60

About This Book

Choose from 12 featured sweaters!

From sleeve styles and necklines to closures and edgings, this is a book of choices, to help you create adorable sweaters for babies and kids. We start by presenting 12 complete sweater designs, to show you some of the possible combinations. The instructions are written in the traditional beginning-to-end format, with no need to make choices or look through each chapter of options. Nearly every option is used in these garments, so you can see how the different details look.

Or pick the pieces for a customized sweater!

This is the absolute easiest way to get started on customizing sweaters for children! This book allows you to knit dozens of sweaters using so many combinations of pieces—without the math or difficulty of designing it yourself! Beginning on page 79, each sweater piece has its own chapter. To create your unique sweater, choose your favorite style of each piece. If you want a cardigan, choose that option. Then choose the sleeves, closure, and collar—and so on. All of the pieces are interchangeable!

Share how to care for your gift!

If the sweater is a gift, it's nice to include the washing information for the yarn used. A gift tag to copy and fill out is provided on page 128 for this purpose.

Record the memories!

Also on page 128, you'll find a project journal to keep a record of the sweaters you create. If you like, attach a photo of that darling child wearing the special sweater you made.

Why knit for babies and kids?

Because they're the most fun people to knit for! Yes, they grow quickly, but sweaters in their little sizes also knit up quickly! And caring for children's sweaters isn't a problem, because many of today's yarns are washable. What's more, the designs included can be knit to fit every size from 6 months to 6 years.

Enjoy the creativity!

I hope you find endless joy in creating these adorable sweaters. I had fun developing each element and would like to thank my helpers: Lori Kerby, Joe Miser, Elizabeth Miser, and Deanna Miser.

—Lorna Miser

Buttoned V-Neck Cardigan

◼◼◻◻ EASY +

FEATURED DETAILS

- Garter Stitch Edging
- Seed Stitch fabric
- V-Neck Cardigan
- Cap Sleeves
- Patch Pockets
- Garter Stitch Band
- Button closure

SHOPPING LIST

Yarn (Medium Weight)
[3.5 ounces, 207 yards
(100 grams, 188 meters) per skein]:
☐ {2-3-3}{3-4-4} skeins

Knitting Needles
☐ Straight needles, size 6 (4 mm)
☐ Double pointed needles, size 6 (4 mm)
☐ 24-36" (61-91.5 cm) circular needle,
size 6 (4 mm)
or sizes needed for gauge

Additional Supplies
☐ Point protectors for circular needle
☐ Markers - split ring, locked, or scrap yarn
☐ Yarn needle
☐ Sewing needle and thread
☐ ⁵⁄₈" (16 mm) Buttons - {3-4-4}{4-5-6}
☐ Pins

SIZE INFORMATION

Sizes	Finished Chest Measurement	
6 months	20¹⁄₂"	(52 cm)
12 months	22¹⁄₄"	(56.5 cm)
18 months	23³⁄₄"	(60.5 cm)
2 years	25¹⁄₄"	(64 cm)
4 years	28¹⁄₄"	(72 cm)
6 years	30¹⁄₄"	(77 cm)

Size Note: We have printed the instructions
for the sizes in different colors to make it
easier for you to find:
- 6 months in Purple
- 12 months in Lt Blue
- 18 months in Pink
- 2 years in Orange
- 4 years in Blue
- 6 years in Green

Instructions in black apply to all sizes.

GAUGE INFORMATION

In Seed Stitch (Rows 1 and 2 of Back Body),
21 sts and 30 rows = 4¹⁄₄" (10.75 cm)

TECHNIQUES USED
- YO *(Fig. 3a, page 122)*
- K2 tog *(Fig. 7, page 124)*
- SSK *(Figs. 8a-c, page 124)*

BODY

Row 1 (Right side): K2, P1, (K1, P1) across to last 2 sts, K2.

Row 2: P1, (K1, P1) across.

Note: Loop a short piece of yarn around any stitch to mark Row 2 as **right** side.

Repeat Rows 1 and 2 for Seed Stitch until Back measures approximately {6-7-8}{9-10-11}"/ {15-18-20.5}{23-25.5-28} cm from cast on edge.

Note: Place a marker around the first and last stitch to indicate Sleeve placement *(see Markers, page 121).*

Continue working in Seed Stitch until Back measures approximately {4¹/₂-5-5¹/₂}{6-6¹/₂-7}"/ {11.5-12.5-14}{15-16.5-18} cm from markers, ending by working a **wrong** side row (Row 2); cut yarn.

Slip all sts onto a circular needle; place point protectors on needle. The Back will be joined to the Fronts at the shoulders using 3-needle bind off.

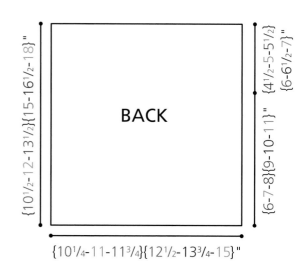

{10¹/₂-12-13¹/₂}{15-16¹/₂-18}"

{4¹/₂-5-5¹/₂}{6-6¹/₂-7}"

BACK

{6-7-8}{9-10-11}"

{10¹/₄-11-11³/₄}{12¹/₂-13³/₄-15}"

BACK
GARTER STITCH EDGING

Using straight needles, cast on {51-55-59} {63-69-75} sts.

Knit 6 rows.

LEFT FRONT
GARTER STITCH EDGING
Using straight needles, cast on {25-27-29}
{31-35-37} sts.

Knit 6 rows.

BODY
Work in Seed Stitch same as Back until Front
measures approximately {6-7-8}{9-10-11}"/
{15-18-20.5}{23-25.5-28} cm from cast on edge,
ending by working a **wrong** side row (Row 2).

Note: Place a marker around the first and last
stitch to indicate Sleeve and Garter Stitch Band
placement.

V-NECK SHAPING
Maintain established Seed Stitch throughout.

Sizes 6, 12, & 18 Months ONLY
Row 1 (Decrease row): Work across to last 2 sts,
SSK: {24-26-28} sts.

Row 2: Work across.

Repeat Rows 1 and 2, {10-11-12} times:
{14-15-16} sts.

Sizes 2, 4, & 6 ONLY
Row 1 (Decrease row): Work across to last 2 sts,
SSK: {30-34-36} sts.

Row 2: Work across.

Row 3 (Decrease row): Work across to last 2 sts,
SSK: {29-33-35} sts.

Rows 4-6: Work across.

Repeat Rows 1-6, {5-6-6} times; then repeat Row 1,
{1-1-0} time(s) **more** *(see Zeros, page 121)*:
{18-20-23} sts.

All Sizes
Work even until Front measures same as Back,
ending by working a **wrong** side row; do **not**
cut yarn.

With **right** sides together and Back in front of
Front, work 3-needle bind off to join the Left Front
and Back shoulders *(Fig. 12, page 125)*.

RIGHT FRONT
Work same as Left Front to V-Neck Shaping:
{25-27-29}{31-35-37} sts.

Note: Place a marker around the first and
last stitch to indicate Sleeve and Garter Stitch
Band placement.

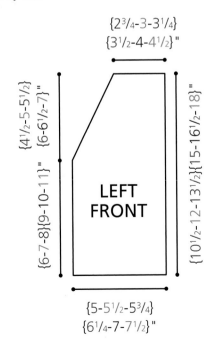

{2³/₄-3-3¹/₄}
{3¹/₂-4-4¹/₂}"

{4¹/₂-5-5¹/₂}
{6-6¹/₂-7}"

{10¹/₂-12-13¹/₂}{15-16¹/₂-18}"

{6-7-8}{9-10-11}"

LEFT FRONT

{5-5¹/₂-5³/₄}
{6¹/₄-7-7¹/₂}"

V-NECK SHAPING

Maintain established Seed Stitch throughout.

Sizes 6, 12, & 18 Months ONLY

Row 1 (Decrease row): K2 tog, work across: {24-26-28} sts.

Row 2: Work across.

Repeat Rows 1 and 2, {10-11-12} times: {14-15-16} sts.

Sizes 2, 4, & 6 ONLY

Row 1 (Decrease row): K2 tog, work across: {30-34-36} sts.

Row 2: Work across.

Row 3 (Decrease row): K2 tog, work across: {29-33-35} sts.

Rows 4-6: Work across.

Repeat Rows 1-6, {5-6-6} times; then repeat Row 1, {1-1-0} time(s) **more**: {18-20-23} sts.

All Sizes

Work even until Front measures same as Back, ending by working a **wrong** side row; do **not** cut yarn.

Slip {14-15-16}{18-20-23} right shoulder sts from Back neck circular needle onto a straight needle, leaving remaining {23-25-27}{27-29-29} neck sts on circular needle. Using a double pointed needle, work 3-needle bind off to join the Right Front and Back shoulders.

CAP SLEEVE

With **right** side of Body facing and using straight needles, pick up {45-51-55}{61-65-71} sts evenly spaced between markers *(Fig. 11a, page 125)*; remove markers.

Row 1: P1, (K1, P1) across.

Row 2 (Decrease row): K2 tog, P1, (K1, P1) across to last 2 sts, SSK: {43-49-53}{59-63-69} sts.

Row 3: K1, (P1, K1) across.

Row 4 (Decrease row): K2 tog, K1, (P1, K1) across to last 2 sts, SSK: {41-47-51}{57-61-67} sts.

Rows 5 and 6: Repeat Rows 1 and 2: {39-45-49}{55-59-65} sts.

Knit 6 rows for Garter Stitch Edging.

Bind off all sts in **knit**.

Repeat for second Cap Sleeve.

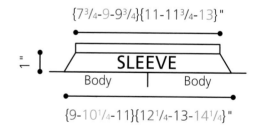

{7³⁄₄-9-9³⁄₄}{11-11³⁄₄-13}"

SLEEVE

Body | Body

{9-10¹⁄₄-11}{12¹⁄₄-13-14¹⁄₄}"

PATCH POCKET (Make 2)

Using straight needles, cast on {15-15-20} {20-20-20} sts.

Knit every row until Pocket measures approximately {3-3-4}{4-4-4}"/{7.5-7.5-10}{10-10-10} cm from cast on edge.

Bind off all sts in **knit** leaving a long end for sewing.

Using photo as a guide for placement, page 7, pin Pockets to Front, then sew in place.

FINISHING

Weave underarm and side in one continuous seam, one half stitch in *(Fig. 13, page 125)*.

GARTER STITCH BAND

With **right** side facing, using circular needle (holding Back neck sts) and beginning at Right Front Edging, pick up {29-35-41}{47-53-55} sts evenly spaced across to marker, remove marker, pick up {22-24-26}{28-30-32} sts evenly spaced across neck edge to shoulder, knit {23-25-27} {27-29-29} sts across Back neck, pick up {22-24-26} {28-30-32} sts evenly spaced across Left Front neck edge to marker, remove marker for Girl's Band **only**, pick up {29-35-41}{47-53-55} sts evenly spaced across: {125-143-161}{177-195-203} sts.

Rows 1-3: Knit across.

Girl's Sweater Only - Row 4 (Buttonhole row): K3, YO, K2 tog, ★ K {10-8-10}{12-10-8}, YO, K2 tog; repeat from ★ {1-2-2}{2-3-4} time(s) **more**, knit across.

Boy's Sweater Only - Row 4 (Buttonhole row): Knit across to Left Front marker, YO, K2 tog, ★ K {10-8-10}{12-10-8}, YO, K2 tog; repeat from ★ {1-2-2}{2-3-4} time(s) **more**, K3.

Rows 5-7: Knit across.

Bind off all sts in **knit**.

Sew {3-4-4}{4-5-6} buttons to Front Band to correspond with buttonholes.

Short Sleeve Topper

◼◼◼◻◻ **EASY +**

FEATURED DETAILS

- Picots Edging
- Seed Stitch fabric
- V-Neck Cardigan
- Short Sleeves
- Garter Stitch Band
- Tie closure

SHOPPING LIST

Yarn (Medium Weight) 🄴 4
[3.5 ounces, 180 yards
(100 grams, 165 meters) per hank]:
☐ {2-2-3}{3-4-4} hanks

Knitting Needles
☐ Straight needles, size 6 (4 mm)
☐ Double pointed needles, size 6 (4 mm)
☐ 24-36" (61-91.5 cm) circular needle,
   size 6 (4 mm)
   or sizes needed for gauge

Additional Supplies
☐ Point protectors for circular needle
☐ Markers - split ring, locked, or scrap yarn
☐ Yarn needle

SIZE INFORMATION

Sizes	Finished Chest Measurement	
6 months	21¼"	(54 cm)
12 months	23"	(58.5 cm)
18 months	24½"	(62 cm)
2 years	26"	(66 cm)
4 years	29"	(73.5 cm)
6 years	31"	(78.5 cm)

Size Note: We have printed the instructions for the sizes in different colors to make it easier for you to find:
- 6 months in Purple
- 12 months in Lt blue
- 18 months in Pink
- 2 years in Orange
- 4 years in Blue
- 6 years in Green

Instructions in black apply to all sizes.

GAUGE INFORMATION
In Seed Stitch (Rows 1 and 2 of Back Body),
   21 sts and 30 rows = 4¼" (10.75 cm)

TECHNIQUES USED
- Adding new stitches *(Figs. 4a & b, page 123)*
- K2 tog *(Fig. 7, page 124)*
- SSK *(Figs. 8a-c, page 124)*

BACK
PICOTS EDGING
Using straight needles, place a slip knot on needle, add on 4 sts, bind off 2 sts in **knit**, slip st back onto left needle, ★ add on 5 sts, bind off 2 sts in **knit**, slip st back onto left needle; repeat from ★ until there are {51-54-57}{63-69-75} sts; add on {0-1-2}{0-0-0} st(s) *(see Zeros, page 121)*: {51-55-59}{63-69-75} sts.

BODY
Row 1 (Right side): K2, P1, (K1, P1) across to last 2 sts, K2.

Row 2: P1, (K1, P1) across.

Note: Loop a short piece of yarn around any stitch to mark Row 2 as **right** side.

Repeat Rows 1 and 2 for Seed Stitch until Back measures approximately {6-7-8}{9-10-11}"/{15-18-20.5}{23-25.5-28} cm from bottom edge.

Note: Place a marker around the first and last stitch to indicate Sleeve placement *(see Markers, page 121)*.

Continue working in Seed Stitch until Back measures approximately {4½-5-5½}{6-6½-7}"/{11.5-12.5-14}{15-16.5-18} cm from markers, ending by working a **wrong** side row (Row 2); cut yarn.

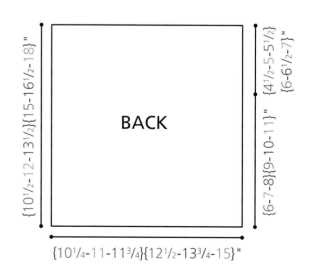

{10½-12-13½}{15-16½-18}"

BACK

{4½-5-5½}{6-6½-7}"

{6-7-8}{9-10-11}"

{10¼-11-11¾}{12½-13¾-15}"

Slip all sts onto a circular needle; place point protectors on needle. The Back will be joined to the Fronts at the shoulders using 3-needle bind off.

LEFT FRONT
PICOTS EDGING
Using straight needles, place a slip knot on needle, add on 4 sts, bind off 2 sts in **knit**, slip st back onto left needle, ★ add on 5 sts, bind off 2 sts in **knit**, slip st back onto left needle; repeat from ★ until there are {24-27-27}{30-33-36} sts; add on {1-0-2}{1-2-1} st(s): {25-27-29}{31-35-37} sts.

BODY
Work in Seed Stitch same as Back until Front measures approximately {6-7-8}{9-10-11}"/{15-18-20.5}{23-25.5-28} cm from bottom edge, ending by working a **wrong** side row (Row 2).

Note: Place a marker around the first and last stitch to indicate Sleeve and Garter Stitch Band placement.

V-NECK SHAPING
Maintain established Seed Stitch throughout.

Sizes 6, 12, & 18 Months ONLY
Row 1 (Decrease row): Work across to last 2 sts, SSK: {24-26-28} sts.

Row 2: Work across.

Repeat Rows 1 and 2, {10-11-12} times: {14-15-16} sts.

Sizes 2, 4, & 6 ONLY
Row 1 (Decrease row): Work across to last 2 sts, SSK: {30-34-36} sts.

Row 2: Work across.

Row 3 (Decrease row): Work across to last 2 sts, SSK: {29-33-35} sts.

Rows 4-6: Work across.

Repeat Rows 1-6, {5-6-6} times; then repeat Row 1, {1-1-0} time(s) **more**: {18-20-23} sts.

All Sizes
Work even until Front measures same as Back, ending by working a **wrong** side row; do **not** cut yarn.

With **right** sides together and Back in front of Front, work 3-needle bind off to join the Left Front and Back shoulders *(Fig. 12, page 125)*.

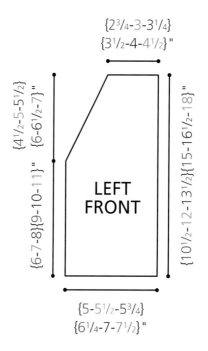

RIGHT FRONT
Work same as Left Front to V-Neck Shaping: {25-27-29}{31-35-37} sts.

Note: Place a marker around the first and last stitch to indicate Sleeve and Garter Stitch Band placement.

V-NECK SHAPING

Maintain established Seed Stitch throughout.

Sizes 6, 12, & 18 Months ONLY

Row 1 (Decrease row): K2 tog, work across: {24-26-28} sts.

Row 2: Work across.

Repeat Rows 1 and 2, {10-11-12} times: {14-15-16} sts.

Sizes 2, 4, & 6 ONLY

Row 1 (Decrease row): K2 tog, work across: {30-34-36} sts.

Row 2: Work across.

Row 3 (Decrease row): K2 tog, work across: {29-33-35} sts.

Rows 4-6: Work across.

Repeat Rows 1-6, {5-6-6} times; then repeat Row 1, {1-1-0} time(s) **more**: {18-20-23} sts.

All Sizes

Work even until Front measures same as Back, ending by working a **wrong** side row; do **not** cut yarn.

Slip {14-15-16}{18-20-23} right shoulder sts from Back neck circular needle onto a straight needle, leaving remaining {23-25-27}{27-29-29} neck sts on circular needle. Using a double pointed needle, work 3-needle bind off to join the Right Front and Back shoulders.

SHORT SLEEVE

With **right** side of Body facing and using straight needles, pick up {45-51-55}{61-65-71} sts evenly spaced between markers (*Fig. 11a, page 125*); remove markers.

Row 1: P1, (K1, P1) across.

Row 2 (Decrease row): K2 tog, P1, (K1, P1) across to last 2 sts, SSK: {43-49-53}{59-63-69} sts.

Row 3: K1, (P1, K1) across.

Row 4 (Decrease row): K2 tog, K1, (P1, K1) across to last 2 sts, SSK: {41-47-51}{57-61-67} sts.

Rows 5-10: Repeat Rows 1-4 once, then repeat Rows 1 and 2 once **more**: {35-41-45}{51-55-61} sts.

Work even until Sleeve measures approximately {2-2½-3}{3½-4-4½}"/{5-6.5-7.5}{9-10-11.5} cm, ending by working a **wrong** side row.

Knit 4 rows for Garter Stitch Edging.

Bind off all sts in **knit**.

Repeat for second Short Sleeve.

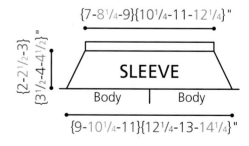

FINISHING

Weave underarm and side in one continuous seam, one half stitch in *(Fig. 13, page 125)*.

GARTER STITCH BAND

With **right** side facing, using circular needle (holding Back neck sts) and beginning at Right Front edging, pick up {29-35-41}{47-53-55} sts evenly spaced across to marker, remove marker, pick up {22-24-26}{28-30-32} sts evenly spaced across neck edge to shoulder, knit {23-25-27}{27-29-29} sts across Back neck, pick up {22-24-26}{28-30-32} sts evenly spaced across Left Front neck edge to marker, remove marker, pick up {29-35-41}{47-53-55} sts evenly spaced across: {125-143-161}{177-195-203} sts.

Knit 3 rows.

Bind off all sts in **knit**.

TIE (Make 2)

Using double pointed needles, cast on 3 sts; ★ do **not** turn, slide sts to opposite end of needle, K3; repeat from ★ until Tie measures approximately 10" (25.5 cm) long.

Cut yarn; thread yarn needle with end and slip sts onto yarn needle; gather tightly to close and secure end; sew Tie to bottom of V-Neck.

Sunshine Pullover with Collar

◧ ▮▮▯▯ EASY +

FEATURED DETAILS

- Rolled Edging
- Broken Rib fabric
- V-Neck Pullover
- Short Sleeves
- Sun Appliqué
- Collar

SIZE INFORMATION

Sizes	Finished Chest Measurement	
6 months	20"	(51 cm)
12 months	21½"	(54.5 cm)
18 months	23¼"	(59 cm)
2 years	24¾"	(63 cm)
4 years	27¼"	(69 cm)
6 years	29½"	(75 cm)

Size Note: We have printed the instructions for the sizes in different colors to make it easier for you to find:
- 6 months in Purple
- 12 months in Lt Blue
- 18 months in Pink
- 2 years in Orange
- 4 years in Blue
- 6 years in Green

Instructions in black apply to all sizes.

GAUGE INFORMATION

In Broken Rib (Rows 1 and 2 of Back Body),
  20 sts and 28 rows = 4" (10 cm)

TECHNIQUES USED

- Adding new stitches *(Figs. 4a & b, page 123)*
- Knit increase *(Figs. 6a & b, page 123)*
- K2 tog *(Fig. 7, page 124)*
- SSK *(Figs. 8a-c, page 124)*

BODY

Begin using Main Color.

Row 1 (Right side): Knit across.

Row 2: P1, (K1, P1) across.

Repeat Rows 1 and 2 for Broken Rib until Back measures approximately {6-7-8}{9-10-11}"/ {15-18-20.5}{23-25.5-28} cm from bottom edge (allowing the Edging to roll).

Note: Place a marker around the first and last stitch to indicate Sleeve placement *(see Markers, page 121).*

Continue working in Broken Rib until Back measures approximately {4½-5-5½}{6-6½-7}"/ {11.5-12.5-14}{15-16.5-18} cm from markers, ending by working a **wrong** side row (Row 2); cut yarn.

Slip all sts onto a circular needle; place point protectors on needle. The Back will be joined to the Front at the shoulders using 3-needle bind off.

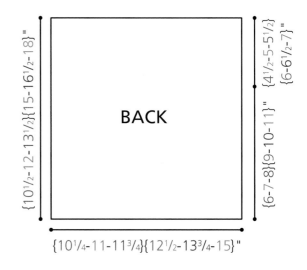

BACK

{10¼-12-13½}{15-16½-18}"

{4½-5-5½}{6-6½-7}"

{6-7-8}{9-10-11}"

{10¼-11-11¾}{12½-13¾-15}"

BACK
ROLLED EDGE

Using straight needles and Contrasting Color, cast on {51-55-59}{63-69-75} sts.

Beginning with a **knit** row, work in Stockinette Stitch (knit one row, purl one row) for 10 rows.

Cut Contrasting Color.

FRONT

Work same as Back until Front measures approximately {6-7-8}{9-10-11}"/{15-18-20.5} {23-25.5-28} cm from bottom edge (allowing the Edging to roll), ending by working a **wrong** side row (Row 2): {51-55-59}{63-69-75} sts.

Note: Place a marker around the first and last stitch to indicate Sleeve placement.

V-NECK SHAPING

Both sides of Neck are worked at the same time using separate yarn for each side. Maintain established Broken Rib throughout.

Row 1: Knit {25-27-29}{31-34-37} sts, slip next st onto st holder for Collar; with second yarn, knit across: {25-27-29}{31-34-37} sts **each** side.

Sizes 6, 12, & 18 Months ONLY

Row 2: Work across; with second yarn, work across.

Row 3 (Decrease row): Knit across to within 2 sts of neck edge, SSK; with second yarn, K2 tog, knit across: {24-26-28} sts **each** side.

Repeat Rows 2 and 3, {10-11-12} times: {14-15-16} sts **each** side.

Sizes 2, 4, & 6 ONLY

Row 2: Work across; with second yarn, work across.

Row 3 (Decrease row): Knit across to within 2 sts of neck edge, SSK; with second yarn, K2 tog, knit across: {30-33-36} sts **each** side.

Rows 4-6: Work across; with second yarn, work across.

Row 7 (Decrease row): Knit across to within 2 sts of neck edge, SSK; with second yarn, K2 tog, knit across: {29-32-35} sts **each** side.

Repeat Rows 2-7, {5-6-6} times; then repeat Rows 2 and 3, {1-0-0} time(s) **more** *(see Zeros, page 121)*: {18-20-23} sts **each** side.

All Sizes

Work even until Front measures same as Back, ending by working a **wrong** side row; do **not** cut yarn.

With **right** sides together and Back in front of Front, work 3-needle bind off to join the left Front and Back shoulders *(Fig. 12, page 125)*.

Slip {14-15-16}{18-20-23} right shoulder sts from Back neck circular needle onto a straight needle, leaving remaining {23-25-27}{27-29-29} neck sts on circular needle. Using a double pointed needle, work 3-needle bind off to join the right Front and Back shoulders.

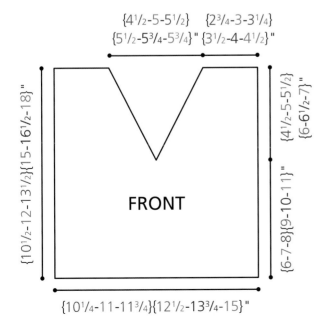

{4¹⁄₂-5-5¹⁄₂} {2³⁄₄-3-3¹⁄₄}
{5¹⁄₂-5³⁄₄-5³⁄₄}" {3¹⁄₂-4-4¹⁄₂}"

{10¹⁄₂-12-13¹⁄₂}{15-16¹⁄₂-18}"

{4¹⁄₂-5-5¹⁄₂}
{6-6¹⁄₂-7}"

{6-7-8}{9-10-11}"

FRONT

{10¹⁄₄-11-11³⁄₄}{12¹⁄₂-13³⁄₄-15}"

SHORT SLEEVE

With **right** side of Body facing, using straight needles and Main Color, pick up {45-51-55} {61-65-71} sts evenly spaced between markers *(Fig. 11a, page 125)*; remove markers.

Row 1: P1, (K1, P1) across.

Row 2 (Decrease row): K2 tog, knit across to last 2 sts, SSK: {43-49-53}{59-63-69} sts.

Row 3: K1, (P1, K1) across.

Row 4 (Decrease row): K2 tog, knit across to last 2 sts, SSK: {41-47-51}{57-61-67} sts.

Rows 5-10: Repeat Rows 1-4 once, then repeat Rows 1 and 2 once **more**: {35-41-45} {51-55-61} sts.

Row 11: K1, (P1, K1) across.

Row 12: Knit across.

Repeat Rows 11 and 12 until Sleeve measures approximately {2-2½-3}{3½-4-4½}"/{5-6.5-7.5} {9-10-11.5} cm, ending by working a **wrong** side row (Row 11).

Cut Main Color; using Contrasting Color and beginning with a **knit** row, work in Stockinette Stitch for 10 rows for a Rolled Edge.

Bind off all sts in **knit**.

Repeat for second Short Sleeve.

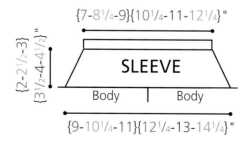

SUN APPLIQUÉ

Using double pointed needles *(Figs. 2a & b, page 121)* and Contrasting Color, cast on 8 sts.

Foundation Row: Purl across dividing sts onto 3 needles, arranged 3-3-2.

Begin working in rounds.

Rnd 1 (Right side): Knit increase in each st around; place marker around first stitch to indicate beginning of rnds: 16 sts.

Rnds 2 and 3: Knit around.

Rnd 4: Knit increase in each st around: 32 sts.

Rnds 5-8: Knit around.

Rnd 9: ★ Add on 2 sts, bind off 5 sts in **knit**, slip st back onto left needle; repeat from ★ around to last 5 sts, add on 2 sts, bind off remaining sts leaving a long end for sewing.

Block appliqué so it lays flat *(see Blocking, page 126)*.

Using photo as a guide and Black embroidery floss, embroider face using French knots for eyes and backstitch for the mouth *(see Embroidery Stitches, page 126)*.

Using photo as a guide for placement, pin appliqué to sweater, then sew in place.

FINISHING

Weave underarm and side in one continuous seam, one half stitch in *(Fig. 13, page 125)*.

COLLAR

With **wrong** side facing, using circular needle (holding Back neck sts) and Contrasting Color, slip center st from Front st holder onto needle and purl it, pick up one st on Left Front neck edge, pass center st over the picked up st and off the needle, pick up {21-23-25}{27-29-31} sts evenly spaced along left Front neck edge, knit {23-25-27} {27-29-29} sts across Back neck, pick up {22-24-26} {28-30-32} sts evenly spaced along right Front neck edge; do **not** join: {67-73-79}{83-89-93} sts.

Knit every row for 3" (7.5 cm).

Bind off all sts **loosely** in **knit**.

Ruffled Topper

EASY +

FEATURED DETAILS

- Ruffle Edging
- Seed Stitch fabric
- Crewneck Cardigan
- Cap Sleeves
- Garter Stitch Front and Neck Bands
- Tie closure

SHOPPING LIST

Yarn (Medium Weight)
[3.5 ounces, 207 yards
(100 grams, 188 meters) per skein]:
- ☐ Main Color (Dk Rose) - {2-2-2}{3-3-3} skeins
- ☐ Contrasting Color (Rose) - {1-1-1}{1-2-2} skein(s)

Knitting Needles
- ☐ Straight needles, size 6 (4 mm)
- ☐ Double pointed needles, size 6 (4 mm)
- ☐ 24-36" (61-91.5 cm) circular needle, size 6 (4 mm)
  or sizes needed for gauge

Additional Supplies
- ☐ Point protectors for circular needle
- ☐ Markers - split ring, locked, or scrap yarn
- ☐ Yarn needle

SIZE INFORMATION

Sizes	Finished Chest Measurement	
6 months	21¼"	(54 cm)
12 months	23"	(58.5 cm)
18 months	24½"	(62 cm)
2 years	26"	(66 cm)
4 years	29"	(73.5 cm)
6 years	31"	(78.5 cm)

Size Note: We have printed the instructions for the sizes in different colors to make it easier for you to find:
- 6 months in Purple
- 12 months in Lt Blue
- 18 months in Pink
- 2 years in Orange
- 4 years in Blue
- 6 years in Green

Instructions in black apply to all sizes.

GAUGE INFORMATION
In Seed Stitch (Rows 1 and 2 of Back Body),
  21 sts and 30 rows = 4¼" (10.75 cm)

TECHNIQUES USED
- Knit increase *(Figs. 6a & b, page 123)*
- K2 tog *(Fig. 7, page 124)*
- SSK *(Figs. 8a-c, page 124)*
- P2 tog *(Fig. 10, page 124)*

BACK
RUFFLE EDGING

Using straight needles and Contrasting Color, cast on {102-110-118}{126-138-150} sts.

Rows 1-5: Knit across (Garter Stitch).

Row 6: Purl across.

Row 7 (Right side): Knit across.

Rows 8-11: Repeat Rows 6 and 7 twice.

Row 12: P2 tog across; cut Contrasting Color: {51-55-59}{63-69-75} sts.

BODY

Row 1: Using Main Color, knit across.

Row 2: P1, (K1, P1) across.

Row 3: K2, P1, (K1, P1) across to last 2 sts, K2.

Repeat Rows 2 and 3 for Seed Stitch until Back measures approximately {6-7-8}{9-10-11}"/ {15-18-20.5}{23-25.5-28} cm from cast on edge.

Note: Place a marker around the first and last stitch to indicate Sleeve placement *(see Markers, page 121).*

Continue working in Seed Stitch until Back measures approximately {4½-5-5½}{6-6½-7}"/ {11.5-12.5-14}{15-16.5-18} cm from markers, ending by working a **wrong** side row (Row 2); cut yarn.

Slip all sts onto a circular needle; place point protectors on needle. The Back will be joined to the Fronts at the shoulders using 3-needle bind off.

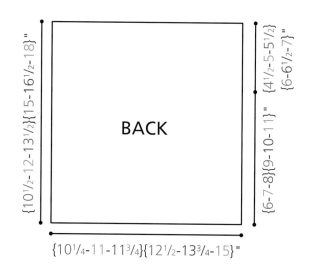

{10½-12-13½}{15-16½-18}"

{4½-5-5½}{6-6½-7}"

BACK

{6-7-8}{9-10-11}"

{10¼-11-11¾}{12½-13¾-15}"

LEFT FRONT
RUFFLE EDGING
Using straight needles and Contrasting Color, cast on {50-54-58}{62-70-74} sts.

Rows 1-5: Knit across.

Row 6: Purl across.

Row 7 (Right side): Knit across.

Rows 8-11: Repeat Rows 6 and 7 twice.

Row 12: P2 tog across; cut Contrasting Color: {25-27-29}{31-35-37} sts.

BODY
Row 1: Using Main Color, knit across.

Work in Seed Stitch same as Back until Front measures approximately {6-7-8}{9-10-11}"/ {15-18-20.5}{23-25.5-28} cm from cast on edge.

Note: Place a marker around stitch at side edge to indicate Sleeve placement.

Work even until Front measures approximately {8½-10-11½}{13-14½-16}"/{21.5-25.5-29} {33-37-40.5} cm from cast on edge, ending by working a **right** side row (Row 3).

CREWNECK SHAPING
Maintain established pattern throughout.

Row 1: Bind off {5-6-7}{7-9-8} sts, work across: {20-21-22}{24-26-29} sts.

Row 2: Work across.

Row 3 (Decrease row): Bind off 2 sts, work across: {18-19-20}{22-24-27} sts.

Rows 4-7: Repeat Rows 2 and 3 twice: {14-15-16}{18-20-23} sts.

Work even until Front measures same as Back, ending by working a **wrong** side row; do **not** cut yarn.

With **right** sides together and Back in front of Front, work 3-needle bind off to join the Left Front and Back shoulders *(Fig. 12, page 125)*.

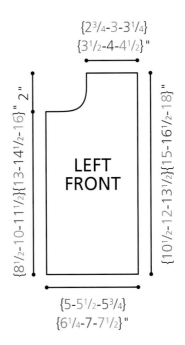

{2¾-3-3¼}
{3½-4-4½}"

{8½-10-11½}{13-14½-16}" 2"

LEFT FRONT

{10½-12-13½}{15-16½-18}"

{5-5½-5¾}
{6¼-7-7½}"

RIGHT FRONT
Work same as Left Front to Crewneck Shaping, ending by working a **wrong** side row (Row 2); then work Crewneck Shaping same as Left Front.

Slip {14-15-16}{18-20-23} right shoulder sts from Back neck circular needle onto a straight needle, leaving remaining {23-25-27}{27-29-29} neck sts on circular needle. Using a double pointed needle, work 3-needle bind off to join the Right Front and Back shoulders.

CAP SLEEVE

With **right** side of Body facing, using straight needles and Main Color, pick up {45-51-55} {61-65-71} sts evenly spaced between markers *(Fig. 11a, page 125)*; remove markers.

Row 1: P1, (K1, P1) across.

Row 2 (Decrease row): K2 tog, P1, (K1, P1) across to last 2 sts, SSK: {43-49-53}{59-63-69} sts.

Row 3: K1, (P1, K1) across.

Row 4 (Decrease row): K2 tog, K1, (P1, K1) across to last 2 sts, SSK: {41-47-51}{57-61-67} sts.

Rows 5-7: Repeat Rows 1-3: {39-45-49} {55-59-65} sts.

Cut Main Color.

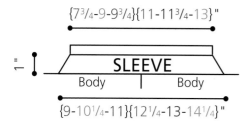

{7¾-9-9¾}{11-11¾-13}"

1"

SLEEVE

Body | Body

{9-10¼-11}{12¼-13-14¼}"

RUFFLE EDGING

Row 1: Using Contrasting Color, knit increase in each st across: {78-90-98}{110-118-130} sts.

Beginning with a **purl** row, work 7 rows in Stockinette Stitch.

Knit 4 rows.

Bind off all sts in **knit**.

Repeat for second Cap Sleeve

FINISHING

Weave underarm and side in one continuous seam, one half stitch in *(Fig. 13, page 125)*.

GARTER STITCH FRONT BAND

With **right** side facing, using straight needles and Contrasting Color, pick up {41-49-57}{65-71-79} sts evenly spaced along one Front edge.

Knit 7 rows.

Bind off all sts in **knit**.

Repeat for second Front.

GARTER STITCH NECK BAND

With **right** side facing, using circular needle (holding Back neck sts), and Contrasting Color, pick up 4 sts across Right Front Band and {5-6-7} {7-9-8} sts across bound off sts *(Fig. 11b, page 125)*, pick up 10 sts evenly spaced along neck edge, knit {23-25-27}{27-29-29} sts across Back neck, pick up 10 sts evenly spaced along Left Front neck edge, pick up {5-6-7}{7-9-8} sts across bound off sts and 4 sts across Front Band: {61-65-69}{69-75-73} sts.

Knit 5 rows.

Bind off all sts **loosely** in **knit**.

TIE (Make 2)

Using double pointed needles and Contrasting Color, cast on 3 sts; ★ do **not** turn, slide sts to opposite end of needle, K3; repeat from ★ until Tie measures approximately 10" (25.5 cm) long.

Cut yarn; thread yarn needle with end and slip sts onto yarn needle; gather tightly to close and secure end; sew Tie to Neck Band.

V-Neck Pullover with Pockets

⬛⬛◻◻◻ EASY +

FEATURED DETAILS

- Garter Stitch Edging
- Stockinette Stitch fabric
- V-Neck Pullover
- Long Sleeves
- Patch Pockets
- Garter Stitch Neck Band

SHOPPING LIST

Yarn (Medium Weight)
[3.5 ounces, 215 yards
(100 grams, 197 meters) per skein]:
☐ {2-2-2}{2-3-3} skeins

Knitting Needles
☐ Straight needles, size 6 (4 mm)
☐ Double pointed needles, size 6 (4 mm)
☐ 24-36" (61-91.5 cm) circular needle, size 6 (4 mm)
or sizes needed for gauge

Additional Supplies
☐ Point protectors for circular needle
☐ Stitch holder
☐ Markers - split ring, locked, or scrap yarn
☐ Yarn needle
☐ Pins

SIZE INFORMATION

Sizes	Finished Chest Measurement	
6 months	20 "	(51 cm)
12 months	21½ "	(54.5 cm)
18 months	23¼ "	(59 cm)
2 years	24¾ "	(63 cm)
4 years	27¼ "	(69 cm)
6 years	29½ "	(75 cm)

Size Note: We have printed the instructions for the sizes in different colors to make it easier for you to find:
- 6 months in Purple
- 12 months in Lt Blue
- 18 months in Pink
- 2 years in Orange
- 4 years in Blue
- 6 years in Green

Instructions in black apply to all sizes.

GAUGE INFORMATION

In Stockinette Stitch (knit one row, purl one row),
20 sts and 28 rows = 4 " (10 cm)

TECHNIQUES USED

- K2 tog *(Fig. 7, page 124)*
- SSK *(Figs. 8a-c, page 124)*
- Slip 2 tog as if to **knit**, K1, P2SSO *(Figs. 9a & b, page 124)*

BACK
GARTER STITCH EDGING
Using straight needles, cast on {51-55 59} {63-69-75} sts.

Knit 6 rows.

BODY
Beginning with a **knit** row, work in Stockinette Stitch until Back measures approximately {6-7-8} {9-10-11}"/{15-18-20.5}{23-25.5-28} cm from cast on edge.

Note: Place a marker around the first and last stitch to indicate Sleeve placement *(see Markers, page 121).*

Continue working in Stockinette Stitch until Back measures approximately {4½-5-5½}{6-6½-7}"/ {11.5-12.5-14}{15-16.5-18} cm from markers, ending by working a **purl** row; cut yarn.

Slip all sts onto a circular needle; place point protectors on needle. The Back will be joined to the Front at the shoulders using 3-needle bind off.

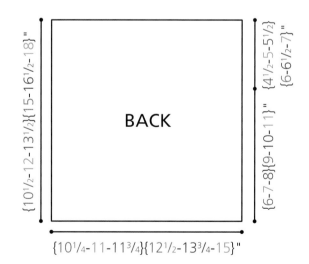

{10½-12-13½}{15-16½-18}"   {4½-5-5½}{6-6½-7}"

BACK

{6-7-8}{9-10-11}"

{10¼-11-11¾}{12½-13¾-15}"

FRONT

Work same as Back until Front measures approximately {6-7-8}{9-10-11}"/{15-18-20.5}{23-25.5-28} cm from cast on edge, ending by working a **purl** row: {51-55-59}{63-69-75} sts.

Note: Place a marker around the first and last stitch to indicate Sleeve placement.

V-NECK SHAPING

Both sides of Neck are worked at the same time using separate yarn for **each** side.

Row 1: Knit {25-27-29}{31-34-37} sts, slip next st onto st holder for Neck Band; with second yarn, knit across: {25-27-29}{31-34-37} sts **each** side.

Sizes 6, 12, & 18 Months ONLY

Row 2: Purl across; with second yarn, purl across.

Row 3 (Decrease row): Knit across to within 3 sts of neck edge, SSK, K1; with second yarn, K1, K2 tog, knit across: {24-26-28} sts **each** side.

Repeat Rows 2 and 3, {10-11-12} times: {14-15-16} sts **each** side.

Sizes 2, 4, & 6 ONLY

Row 2: Purl across; with second yarn, purl across.

Row 3 (Decrease row): Knit across to within 3 sts of neck edge, SSK, K1; with second yarn, K1, K2 tog, knit across: {30-33-36} sts **each** side.

Rows 4-6: Work across; with second yarn, work across.

Row 7 (Decrease row): Knit across to within 3 sts of neck edge, SSK, K1; with second yarn, K1, K2 tog, knit across: {29-32-35} sts **each** side.

Repeat Rows 2-7, {5-6-6} times; then repeat Rows 2 and 3, {1, 0, 0} time(s) **more** *(see Zeros, page 121)*: {18-20-23} sts **each** side.

All Sizes

Work even until Front measures same as Back, ending by working a **purl** row; do **not** cut yarn.

With **right** sides together and Back in front of Front, work 3-needle bind off to join the left Front and Back shoulders *(Fig. 12, page 125)*.

Slip {14-15-16}{18-20-23} right shoulder sts from Back neck circular needle onto a straight needle, leaving remaining {23-25-27}{27-29-29} neck sts on circular needle. Using a double pointed needle, work 3-needle bind off to join the right Front and Back shoulders.

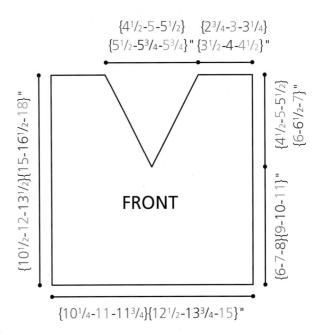

LONG SLEEVE

With **right** side of Body facing and using straight needles, pick up {45-51-55}{61-65-71} sts evenly spaced between markers *(Fig. 11a, page 125)*; remove markers.

Row 1: Purl across.

Row 2: Knit across.

Row 3: Purl across.

Row 4 (Decrease row): K1, K2 tog, knit across to last 3 sts, SSK, K1: {43-49-53}{59-63-69} sts.

Repeat Rows 1-4, {9-11-11}{13-14-16} times: {25-27-31}{33-35-37} sts.

Work even until Sleeve measures approximately {6-7-8}{10-12-14}"/{15-18-20.5} {25.5-30.5-35.5} cm or ³/4" (2 cm) less than desired length, ending by working a **purl** row.

Knit 6 rows for Garter Stitch Edging.

Bind off all sts **loosely** in **knit**.

Repeat for second Long Sleeve.

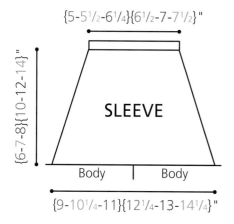

{5-5¹/₂-6¹/₄}{6¹/₂-7-7¹/₂}"

{6-7-8}{10-12-14}"

SLEEVE

Body | Body

{9-10¹/₄-11}{12¹/₄-13-14¹/₄}"

PATCH POCKET (Make 2)

Using straight needles, cast on {15-15-20} {20-20-20} sts.

Knit every row until Pocket measures approximately {3-3-4}{4-4-4}"/{7.5-7.5-10}{10-10-10} cm from cast on edge.

Bind off all sts in **knit** leaving a long end for sewing.

Using photo as a guide for placement, pin Pockets to Front, then sew in place.

FINISHING

Weave underarm and side in one continuous seam, one half stitch in *(Fig. 13, page 125)*.

GARTER STITCH NECK BAND

With **right** side facing, using double pointed needles *(Fig. 2b, page 121)* and placing approximately {23-25-27}{28-30-31} sts on each of 3 needles, knit {23-25-27}{27-29-29} sts across Back neck circular needle, pick up {22-24-26} {28-30-32} sts evenly spaced along left Front neck edge, slip center st from st holder onto empty needle and knit it, place marker around center st, pick up {22-24-26}{28-30-32} sts evenly spaced along right Front neck edge; place marker around first st to indicate beginning of rnd: {68-74-80} {84-90-94} sts.

Rnd 1: Purl across to marked st, K1, purl across.

Rnd 2 (Decrease rnd): Knit across to within one st of marked st, slip 2 tog as if to **knit**, K1, P2SSO, knit across: {66-72-78}{82-88-92} sts.

Rnds 3-6: Repeat Rnds 1 and 2 twice: {62-68-74} {78-84-88} sts.

Bind off remaining sts **loosely** in **purl**.

Lace Top with a Cat

◼◼◻◻ **EASY +**

FEATURED DETAILS

- Lace Edging
- Stockinette Stitch fabric
- Crewneck Pullover
- Boxy Sleeves
- Cat Appliqué
- Garter Stitch Neck Band

SHOPPING LIST

Yarn (Medium Weight) 🌀 **4**
[3.5 ounces, 197 yards
(100 grams, 180 meters) per skein]:
- ☐ Main Color (Red) - {2-2-2}{2-3-3} skeins
- ☐ Contrasting Color (White) - 1 skein
- ☐ Black (for cat) - small amount

Knitting Needles
- ☐ Straight needles, size 6 (4 mm)
- ☐ Double pointed needles, size 6 (4 mm)
- ☐ 24-36" (61-91.5 cm) circular needle, size 6 (4 mm)
  or sizes needed for gauge

Additional Supplies
- ☐ Point protectors for circular needle
- ☐ Stitch holder
- ☐ Markers - split ring, locked, or scrap yarn
- ☐ Yarn needle
- ☐ Pins

SIZE INFORMATION

Sizes	Finished Chest Measurement	
6 months	20"	(51 cm)
12 months	21½"	(54.5 cm)
18 months	23¼"	(59 cm)
2 years	24¾"	(63 cm)
4 years	27¼"	(69 cm)
6 years	29½"	(75 cm)

Size Note: We have printed the instructions for the sizes in different colors to make it easier for you to find:
- 6 months in Purple
- 12 months in Lt Blue
- 18 months in Pink
- 2 years in Orange
- 4 years in Blue
- 6 years in Green

Instructions in black apply to all sizes.

GAUGE INFORMATION

In Stockinette Stitch (knit one row, purl one row),
20 sts and 28 rows = 4" (10 cm)

TECHNIQUES USED

- YO and YO twice (*Figs. 3a & d, page 122*)
- Knit increase (*Figs. 6a & b, page 123*)
- K2 tog (*Fig. 7, page 124*)
- P2 tog (*Fig. 10, page 124*)

BACK
LACE EDGING

Using straight needles and Contrasting Color, cast on 5 sts.

When instructed to slip a stitch, always slip as if to **purl**.

Row 1: WYIF slip 1, K2, YO twice, P2 tog: 6 sts.

Row 2 (Right side): YO, K2, P1, K3: 7 sts.

Row 3: WYIF slip 1, K2, P4.

Row 4: WYIB and slipping first st, bind off first 2 sts, knit across: 5 sts.

Repeat Rows 1-4 until Lace measures approximately {10¼-11-11¾}{12½-13¾-15}"/ {26-28-30}{32-35-38} cm from cast on edge, ending by working Row 4.

Bind off first 3 sts in **knit** and remaining sts in **purl**.

BODY

With **right** side of Lace facing and using Main Color, pick up {51-55-59}{63-69-75} sts evenly spaced along straight edge *(Fig. 11a, page 125)*.

Beginning with a **purl** row, work in Stockinette Stitch until Back measures approximately {6-7-8} {9-10-11}"/{15-18-20.5}{23-25.5-28} cm from bottom edge.

Note: Place a marker around the first and last stitch to indicate Sleeve placement *(see Markers, page 121)*.

Continue working in Stockinette Stitch until Back measures approximately {4½-5-5½}{6-6½-7}"/ {11.5-12.5-14}{15-16.5-18} cm from markers, ending by working a **purl** row; cut yarn.

Slip all sts onto a circular needle; place point protectors on needle. The Back will be joined to the Front at the shoulders using 3-needle bind off.

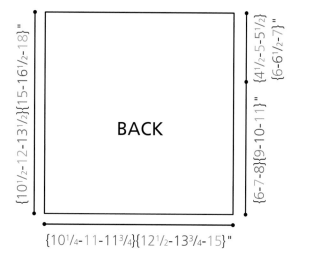

{10½-12-13½}{15-16½-18}"

{6-7-8}{9-10-11}"

{4½-5-5½}{6-6½-7}"

BACK

{10¼-11-11¾}{12½-13¾-15}"

FRONT

Work same as Back until Front measures approximately {8½-10-11½}{13-14½-16}"/{21.5-25.5-29}{33-37-40.5} cm from bottom edge, ending by working a **purl** row: {51-55-59}{63-69-75} sts.

CREWNECK SHAPING

Both sides of Neck are worked at the same time using separate yarn for each side.

Row 1: Knit {20-21-22}{24-26-29} sts; with second yarn, knit across center {11-13-15}{15-17-17} sts and slip these sts onto a st holder; knit across: {20-21-22}{24-26-29} sts **each** side.

Rows 2-7: Work across first side; with second yarn, bind off 2 sts, work across: {14-15-16}{18-20-23} sts **each** side.

Work even until Front measures same as Back, ending by working a **purl** row; do **not** cut yarn.

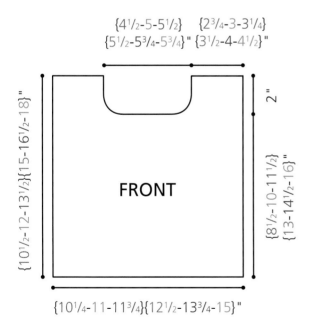

With **right** sides together and Back in front of Front, work 3-needle bind off to join the left Front and Back shoulders *(Fig. 12, page 125)*.

Slip {14-15-16}{18-20-23} right shoulder sts from Back neck circular needle onto a straight needle, leaving remaining {23-25-27}{27-29-29} neck sts on circular needle. Using a double pointed needle, work 3-needle bind off to join the right Front and Back shoulders.

BOXY SLEEVE

With **right** side of Body facing, using straight needles and Main Color, pick up {45-51-55}{61-65-71} sts evenly spaced between markers *(Fig. 11a, page 125)*; remove markers.

Beginning with a **purl** row, work in Stockinette Stitch until Sleeve measures approximately {4-5-6}{8-10-12}"/{10-12.5-15}{20.5-25.5-30.5} cm or 1½" (4 cm) less than desired length, ending by working a **purl** row.

Bind off all sts in **knit**.

Make Lace Edging same as Back until straight edge measures same as bound off edge of Sleeve.

Sew straight edge of Lace Edging to bound off edge of Sleeve.

Repeat for second Boxy Sleeve.

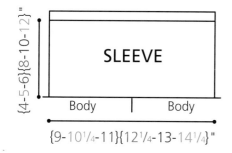

CAT APPLIQUÉ

Using straight needles and Black, cast on 7 sts.

Row 1: Purl across.

Row 2 (Right side - Increase row): Knit increase, knit across to last st, knit increase: 9 sts.

Rows 3-8: Repeat Rows 1 and 2, 3 times: 15 sts.

Row 9: Purl across.

Row 10: Knit across.

Rows 11-15: Repeat Rows 9 and 10 twice, then repeat Row 9 once **more**.

FIRST EAR

Row 1: K6, leave remaining 9 sts unworked; **turn**.

Row 2: P2 tog, P4: 5 sts.

Row 3: K3, K2 tog: 4 sts.

Row 4: P2 tog, P2: 3 sts.

Row 5: K1, K2 tog: 2 sts.

Row 6: P2 tog; cut yarn and pull end through loop.

SECOND EAR

Row 1: With **right** side facing, bind off next 3 sts, knit across: 6 sts.

Row 2: P4, P2 tog: 5 sts.

Row 3: K2 tog, K3: 4 sts.

Row 4: P2, P2 tog: 3 sts.

Row 5: K2 tog, K1: 2 sts.

Row 6: P2 tog; cut yarn leaving a long end for sewing and pull end through loop.

Using photo as a guide and White, embroider face using satin stitch for eyes and nose, and straight stitches for whiskers *(see Embroidery Stitches, page 126)*.

Block appliqué so it lays flat *(see Blocking, page 126)*.

Pin appliqué to sweater; then sew in place.

FINISHING

Weave underarm and side in one continuous seam, one half stitch in *(Fig. 13, page 125)*.

GARTER STITCH NECK BAND

With **right** side facing, using double pointed needles *(Fig. 2b, page 121)*, Main Color, and placing approximately {18-19-21}{21-22-22} sts onto each of 3 needles, knit {23-25-27} {27-29-29} sts across Back neck circular needle, pick up 10 sts evenly spaced along left Front neck edge *(Fig. 11b, page 125)*, knit {11-13-15}{15-17-17} sts from Front neck st holder, pick up 10 sts evenly spaced along right Front neck edge; place marker around first st to indicate beginning of rnd: {54-58-62}{62-66-66} sts.

Rnd 1: Purl around.

Rnd 2: Knit around.

Rnds 3-8: Repeat Rnds 1 and 2, 3 times.

Bind off all sts **loosely** in **purl**.

Star Pocket Pullover

■■☐☐ **EASY +**

FEATURED DETAILS

- Ribbing Edging
- Stockinette Stitch fabric
- Crewneck Pullover
- Long Sleeves
- Large Pullover Pocket
- Star Appliqué
- Neck Ribbing

SHOPPING LIST

Yarn (Medium Weight)
[5 ounces, 256 yards
(141 grams, 234 meters) per skein]:
- ☐ {2-3-3}{3-4-4} skeins
- ☐ Main Color (Green) - {2-2-2}{3-3-3} skeins
- ☐ Contrasting Color (White) - 1 skein

Knitting Needles
- ☐ Straight needles, size 6 (4 mm)
- ☐ Double pointed needles, size 6 (4 mm)
- ☐ 24-36" (61-91.5 cm) circular needle, size 6 (4 mm)
  or sizes needed for gauge

Additional Supplies
- ☐ Point protectors for circular needle
- ☐ Stitch holder
- ☐ Markers - split ring, locked, or scrap yarn
- ☐ Yarn needle
- ☐ Pins

SIZE INFORMATION

Sizes	Finished Chest Measurement	
6 months	20"	(51 cm)
12 months	21½"	(54.5 cm)
18 months	23¼"	(59 cm)
2 years	24¾"	(63 cm)
4 years	27¼"	(69 cm)
6 years	29½"	(75 cm)

Size Note: We have printed the instructions for the sizes in different colors to make it easier for you to find:
- 6 months in Purple
- 12 months in Lt Blue
- 18 months in Pink
- 2 years in Orange
- 4 years in Blue
- 6 years in Green

Instructions in black apply to all sizes.

GAUGE INFORMATION

In Stockinette Stitch (knit one row, purl one row),
  20 sts and 28 rows = 4" (10 cm)

TECHNIQUES USED

- Adding new stitches *(Figs. 4a & b, page 123)*
- K2 tog *(Fig. 7, page 124)*
- SSK *(Figs. 8a-c, page 124)*

Continue working in Stockinette Stitch until Back measures approximately {4½-5-5½}{6-6½-7}"/ {11.5-12.5-14}{15-16.5-18} cm from markers, ending by working a **purl** row; cut yarn.

Slip all sts onto a circular needle; place point protectors on needle. The Back will be joined to the Front at the shoulders using 3-needle bind off.

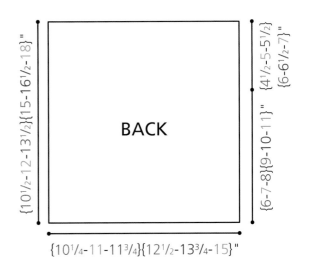

{10½-12-13½}{15-16½-18}"

{6-7-8}{9-10-11}"

{4½-5-5½}{6-6½-7}"

BACK

{10¼-11-11¾}{12½-13¾-15}"

BACK
RIBBING

Using straight needles and Main Color, cast on {51-55-59}{63-69-75} sts.

Row 1 (Right side): K1, (P1, K1) across.

Row 2: P1, (K1, P1) across.

Rows 3-6: Repeat Rows 1 and 2 twice.

BODY

Beginning with a **knit** row, work in Stockinette Stitch until Back measures approximately {6-7-8}{9-10-11}"/{15-18-20.5}{23-25.5-28} cm from cast on edge.

Note: Place a marker around the first and last stitch to indicate Sleeve placement *(see Markers, page 121)*.

FRONT

Work same as Back until Front measures approximately {8½-10-11½}{13-14½-16}"/ {21.5-25.5-29}{33-37-40.5} cm from cast on edge, ending by working a **purl** row: {51-55-59} {63-69-75} sts.

CREWNECK SHAPING

Both sides of Neck are worked at the same time using separate yarn for each side.

Row 1: Knit {20-21-22}{24-26-29} sts; with second yarn, knit across center {11-13-15}{15-17-17} sts and slip these sts onto a st holder; knit across: {20-21-22}{24-26-29} sts **each** side.

Rows 2-7: Work across first side; with second yarn, bind off 2 sts, work across: {14-15-16} {18-20-23} sts **each** side.

Work even until Front measures same as Back, ending by working a **purl** row; do **not** cut yarn.

With **right** sides together and Back in front of Front, work 3-needle bind off to join the left Front and Back shoulders *(Fig. 12, page 125)*.

Slip {14-15-16}{18-20-23} right shoulder sts from Back neck circular needle onto a straight needle, leaving remaining {23-25-27}{27-29-29} neck sts on circular needle. Using a double pointed needle, work 3-needle bind off to join the right Front and Back shoulders.

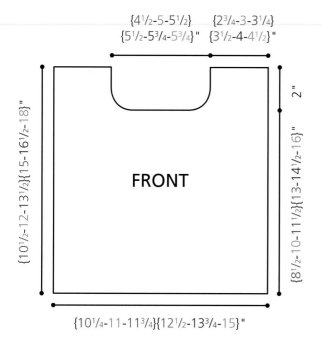

{4½-5-5½}
{5½-5¾-5¾}"   {2¾-3-3¼}
{3½-4-4½}"

2 "

{10½-12-13½}{15-16½-18}"

{8½-10-11½}{13-14½-16}"

FRONT

{10¼-11-11¾}{12½-13¾-15}"

LONG SLEEVE

With **right** side of Body facing, using straight needles and Main Color, pick up {45-51-55} {61-65-71} sts evenly spaced between markers *(Fig.11a, page 125)*; remove markers.

Row 1: Purl across.

Row 2: Knit across.

Row 3: Purl across.

Row 4 (Decrease row): K1, K2 tog, knit across to last 3 sts, SSK, K1: {43-49-53}{59-63-69} sts.

Repeat Rows 1-4, {9-11-11}{13-14-16} times: {25-27-31}{33-35-37} sts.

Work even until Sleeve measures approximately {6-7-8}{10-12-14}"/{15-18-20.5} {25.5-30.5-35.5} cm **or** 1¼" (3 cm) less than desired length, ending by working a **purl** row.

RIBBING
Row 1 (Right side): K1, (P1, K1) across.

Row 2: P1, (K1, P1) across.

Rows 3-6: Repeat Rows 1 and 2 twice.

Bind off all sts **loosely** in pattern.

Repeat for second Sleeve.

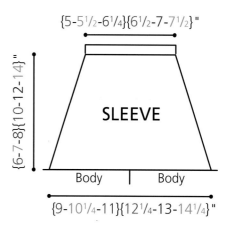

{5-5½-6¼}{6½-7-7½}"

{6-7-8}{10-12-14}"

SLEEVE

Body | Body

{9-10¼-11}{12¼-13-14¼}"

LARGE POCKET

Using straight needles and Main Color, cast on 30 sts.

Knit every row until Pocket measures approximately {3-3-4}{4-4-4}"/{7.5-7.5-10}{10-10-10} cm from cast on edge.

Bind off all sts in **knit** leaving a long end for sewing.

STAR APPLIQUÉ
FIRST POINT

Using double pointed needles and Contrasting Color, place a slip knot on needle, add on 5 sts.

Points are worked in short rows using 2 needles. When instructed to slip a stitch, always slip as if to **purl** with yarn held to **wrong** side.

Row 1 (Right side): Knit across.

Row 2: P3, leave remaining 3 sts unworked; **turn**.

Row 3: Slip 1, K2.

Row 4: P5; **turn**.

Row 5: Slip 1, K4.

Row 6: P3; **turn**.

Row 7: Slip 1, K2.

Row 8: P6.

Row 9: Slipping first st, bind off all sts in **knit**; do **not** cut yarn: one st.

REMAINING 4 POINTS

Add on 5 sts: 6 sts.

Repeat Rows 1-9 of First Point.

CENTER

With **right** side of all Points facing, pick up 4 sts evenly spaced across straight edge of same Point and 5 sts evenly spaced along straight edge of remaining 4 Points: 25 sts.

Divide sts onto 3 double pointed needles, arranged 8-8-9 *(Figs. 2a & b, page 121)*; place marker around first st to indicate beginning of rnd.

Rnd 1: Knit around.

Rnd 2: (SSK, K3) around: 20 sts.

Rnd 3: Knit around.

Rnd 4: (SSK, K2) around: 15 sts.

Rnd 5: Knit around.

Rnd 6: (SSK, K1) around: 10 sts.

Rnd 7: SSK around; cut yarn leaving a long end for sewing: 5 sts.

Thread yarn needle with end and slip remaining sts onto yarn needle; gather tightly to close center and secure end.

Block appliqué so it lays flat *(see Blocking, page 126)*.

Pin appliqué to center of Pocket, then sew in place.

Using photo as a guide for placement, page 43, pin Pocket to Front, then sew in place.

FINISHING
Weave underarm and side in one continuous seam, one half stitch in *(Fig. 13, page 125)*.

NECK RIBBING
With **right** side facing, using double pointed needles, Main Color, and placing approximately {18-19-21}{21-22-22} sts onto each of 3 needles, knit {23-25-27}{27-29-29} sts across Back neck circular needle, pick up 10 sts evenly spaced along left Front neck edge *(Fig. 11b, page 125)*, knit {11-13-15}{15-17-17} sts from Front neck st holder, pick up 10 sts evenly spaced along right Front neck edge; place marker around first st to indicate beginning of rnd: {54-58-62}{62-66-66} sts.

Rnds 1-5: (K1, P1) around.

Bind off all sts **loosely** in pattern.

Zippered Striped Cardi

■■□□ EASY +

FEATURED DETAILS

- Ribbing Edging
- Striped (Stockinette Stitch) fabric
- V-Neck Cardigan
- Short Sleeves
- Ribbing Band
- Zipper closure

SHOPPING LIST

Yarn (Medium Weight) **MEDIUM 4**
[3.5 ounces, 177 yards
(100 grams, 162 meters) per skein]:
☐ Main Color (Blue) - 2 skeins
☐ Contrasting Color (Red) - 2 skeins

Knitting Needles
☐ Straight needles, size 6 (4 mm)
☐ Double pointed needles, size 6 (4 mm)
☐ 24-36" (61-91.5 cm) circular needle,
   size 6 (4 mm)
   or sizes needed for gauge

Additional Supplies
☐ Point protectors for circular needle
☐ Markers - split ring, locked, or scrap yarn
☐ Yarn needle
☐ Sewing needle and thread
☐ Separating zipper - {6-7-8}{9-10-11}"/
   {15-18-20.5}{23-25.5-28} cm **or** longer
   and cut to required length
☐ Pins

SIZE INFORMATION

Sizes	Finished Chest Measurement	
6 months	21³/₄"	(55 cm)
12 months	23¹/₂"	(59.5 cm)
18 months	25"	(63.5 cm)
2 years	26¹/₂"	(67.5 cm)
4 years	29¹/₂"	(75 cm)
6 years	31¹/₂"	(80 cm)

Size Note: We have printed the instructions for the sizes in different colors to make it easier for you to find:
- 6 months in Purple
- 12 months in Lt Blue
- 18 months in Pink
- 2 years in Orange
- 4 years in Blue
- 6 years in Green

Instructions in black apply to all sizes.

GAUGE INFORMATION

In Stockinette Stitch (knit one row, purl one row),
   20 sts and 28 rows = 4" (10 cm)

TECHNIQUES USED

- K2 tog *(Fig. 7, page 124)*
- SSK *(Figs. 8a-c, page 124)*

BODY

Stripe Sequence: ★ 6 Rows of Contrasting Color, 6 rows of Main Color; repeat from ★ for stripe sequence.

Note: Carry unused color loosely along the side edge, twisting colors every 2 rows to prevent long strands along the edge.

Working in stripe sequence and beginning with a **knit** row, work in Stockinette Stitch until Back measures approximately {6-7-8}{9-10-11}"/ {15-18-20.5}{23-25.5-28} cm from cast on edge.

Note: Place a marker around the first and last stitch to indicate Sleeve placement *(see Markers, page 121).*

Continue working in Stockinette Stitch and stripe sequence until Back measures approximately {4¹⁄₂-5-5¹⁄₂}{6-6¹⁄₂-7}"/{11.5-12.5-14} {15-16.5-18} cm from markers, ending by working a **purl** row; cut yarn.

Slip all sts onto a circular needle; place point protectors on needle. The Back will be joined to the Fronts at the shoulders using 3-needle bind off.

BACK
RIBBING

Using straight needles and Main Color, cast on {51-55-59}{63-69-75} sts.

Row 1 (Right side): K1, (P1, K1) across.

Row 2: P1, (K1, P1) across.

Rows 3-6: Repeat Rows 1 and 2 twice.

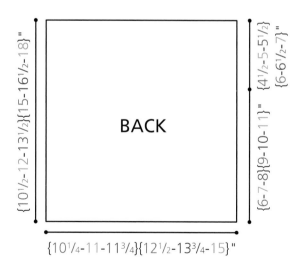

{10¹⁄₂-12-13¹⁄₂}{15-16¹⁄₂-18}"

{4¹⁄₂-5-5¹⁄₂}{6-6¹⁄₂-7}"

BACK

{6-7-8}{9-10-11}"

{10¹⁄₄-11-11³⁄₄}{12¹⁄₂-13³⁄₄-15}"

LEFT FRONT
RIBBING
Using straight needles and Main Color, cast on {25-27-29}{31-35-37} sts.

Row 1 (Right side): K1, (P1, K1) across.

Row 2: P1, (K1, P1) across.

Rows 3-6: Repeat Rows 1 and 2 twice.

BODY
Working in stripe sequence and beginning with a **knit** row, work in Stockinette Stitch until Front measures approximately {6-7-8}{9-10-11}"/ {15-18-20.5}{23-25.5-28} cm from cast on edge, ending by working a **purl** row.

Note: Place a marker around the first and last stitch to indicate Sleeve and Ribbing Band placement.

V-NECK SHAPING
Maintain established stripe sequence throughout.

Sizes 6, 12, & 18 Months ONLY
Row 1 (Decrease row): Knit across to last 3 sts, SSK, K1: {24-26-28} sts.

Row 2: Purl across.

Repeat Rows 1 and 2, {10-11-12} times: {14-15-16} sts.

Sizes 2, 4, & 6 ONLY
Row 1 (Decrease row): Knit across to last 3 sts, SSK, K1: {30-34-36} sts.

Row 2: Purl across.

Row 3 (Decrease row): Knit across to last 3 sts, SSK, K1: {29-33-35} sts.

Row 4: Purl across.

Row 5: Knit across.

Row 6: Purl across.

Repeat Rows 1-6, {5-6-6} times; then repeat Row 1, {1-1-0} time(s) **more** *(see Zeros, page 121)*: {18-20-23} sts.

All Sizes
Work even until Front measures same as Back, ending by working a **purl** row; do **not** cut yarn.

With **right** sides together and Back in front of Front, work 3-needle bind off to join the Left Front and Back shoulders *(Fig. 12, page 125)*.

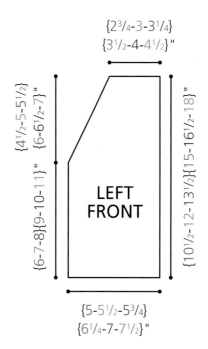

RIGHT FRONT
Work same as Left Front to V-Neck Shaping: {25-27-29}{31-35-37} sts.

Note: Place a marker around the first and last stitch to indicate Sleeve and Ribbing Band placement.

V-NECK SHAPING
Maintain established stripe sequence throughout.

Sizes 6, 12, & 18 Months ONLY
Row 1 (Decrease row): K1, K2 tog, knit across: {24-26-28} sts.

Row 2: Purl across.

Repeat Rows 1 and 2, {10-11-12} times: {14-15-16} sts.

Sizes 2, 4, & 6 ONLY
Row 1 (Decrease row): K1, K2 tog, knit across: {30-34-36} sts.

Row 2: Purl across.

Row 3 (Decrease row): K1, K2 tog, knit across: {29-33-35} sts.

Row 4: Purl across.

Row 5: Knit across.

Row 6: Purl across.

Repeat Rows 1-6, {5-6-6} times; then repeat Row 1, {1-1-0} time(s) **more**: {18-20-23} sts.

All Sizes
Work even until Front measures same as Back, ending by working a **purl** row; do **not** cut yarn.

Slip {14-15-16}{18-20-23} right shoulder sts from Back neck circular needle onto a straight needle, leaving remaining {23-25-27}{27-29-29} neck sts on circular needle. Using a double pointed needle, work 3-needle bind off to join the Right Front and Back shoulders.

SHORT SLEEVE
With **right** side of Body facing, using straight needles and Main Color, pick up {45-51-55}{61-65-71} sts evenly spaced between markers *(Fig. 11a, page 125)*; remove markers.

Stripe Sequence: ★ 6 Rows of Main Color, 6 rows of Contrasting Color; repeat from ★ for stripe sequence.

Row 1: Purl across.

Row 2 (Decrease row): K1, K2 tog, knit across to last 3 sts, SSK, K1: {43-49-53}{59-63-69} sts.

Rows 3-10: Repeat Rows 1 and 2, 4 times: {35-41-45}{51-55-61} sts.

Work even until Sleeve measures approximately {2-2½-3}{3½-4-4½}"/{5-6.5-7.5}{9-10-11.5} cm, ending by working a **purl** row.

Cut Contrasting Color.

RIBBING
Begin using Main Color.

Row 1: K1, (P1, K1) across.

Row 2: P1, (K1, P1) across.

Rows 3-6: Repeat Rows 1 and 2 twice.

Bind off all sts **loosely** in pattern.

Repeat for second Short Sleeve.

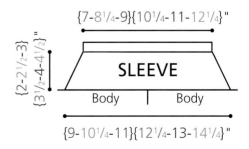

FINISHING

Weave underarm and side in one continuous seam, one half stitch in *(Fig. 13, page 125)*.

RIBBING BAND

With **right** side facing, using circular needle (holding Back neck sts), Main Color, and beginning at Right Front Edging, pick up {29-35-41} {47-53-55} sts evenly spaced across to marker, remove marker, pick up {22-24-26}{28-30-32} sts evenly spaced across neck edge to shoulder, knit {23-25-27}{27-29-29} sts across Back neck, pick up {22-24-26}{28-30-32} sts evenly spaced across Left Front neck edge to marker, remove marker, pick up {29-35-41}{47-53-55} sts evenly spaced across: {125-143-161}{177-195-203} sts.

Row 1: K1, (P1, K1) across.

Row 2: P1, (K1, P1) across.

Rows 3-7: Repeat Rows 1 and 2 twice, then repeat Row 1 once **more**.

Bind off all sts in pattern.

Block cardigan *(see Blocking, page 126)*.

ZIPPER

Pin zipper in place carefully aligning bottom edge of zipper with edging of sweater. If zipper is too long for Front, open zipper, cut zipper length from the top, stitch a heavy zipper stop with thread and fold excess zipper to wrong side. Hand sew zipper in place.

Zippered Heart Hoodie

■■□□ EASY +

FEATURED DETAILS

- Garter Stitch Edging
- Stockinette Stitch fabric
- Crewneck Cardigan
- Boxy Sleeves
- Heart Appliqué
- Garter Stitch Front Band
- Hood
- Zipper closure

SHOPPING LIST

Yarn (Medium Weight) 🧶 MEDIUM 4

[6 ounces, 315 yards (170 grams, 288 meters) per skein]:
- ☐ Main Color (Pink) - {2-2-2}{2-3-3} skeins
- ☐ Contrasting Color (White) - small amount

Knitting Needles

- ☐ Straight needles, size 6 (4 mm)
- ☐ Double pointed needles, size 6 (4 mm)
- ☐ 24-36" (61-91.5 cm) circular needle, size 6 (4 mm)
  or sizes needed for gauge

Additional Supplies

- ☐ Point protectors for circular needle
- ☐ Markers - split ring, locked, or scrap yarn
- ☐ Yarn needle
- ☐ Sewing needle and thread
- ☐ Separating zipper - {8-10-11}{13-14-16}"/ {20.5-25.5-28}{33-35.5-40.5} cm **or** longer and cut to required length
- ☐ Pins

SIZE INFORMATION

Sizes	Finished Chest Measurement	
6 months	21¼"	(54 cm)
12 months	23"	(58.5 cm)
18 months	24½"	(62 cm)
2 years	26"	(66 cm)
4 years	29"	(73.5 cm)
6 years	31"	(78.5 cm)

Size Note: We have printed the instructions for the sizes in different colors to make it easier for you to find:
- 6 months in Purple
- 12 months in Lt Blue
- 18 months in Pink
- 2 years in Orange
- 4 years in Blue
- 6 years in Green

Instructions in black apply to all sizes.

GAUGE INFORMATION

In Stockinette Stitch (knit one row, purl one row),
  20 sts and 28 rows = 4" (10 cm)

TECHNIQUES USED

- M1 (*Figs. 5a & b, page 123*)
- Knit increase (*Figs. 6a & b, page 123*)
- K2 tog (*Fig. 7, page 124*)
- SSK (*Figs. 8a-c, page 124*)

BACK
GARTER STITCH EDGING

Using straight needles and Main Color, cast on {51-55-59}{63-69-75} sts.

Knit 6 rows.

BODY

Beginning with a **knit** row, work in Stockinette Stitch until Back measures approximately {6-7-8}{9-10-11}"/{15-18-20.5}{23-25.5-28} cm from cast on edge.

Note: Place a marker around the first and last stitch to indicate Sleeve placement *(see Markers, page 121)*.

Continue working in Stockinette Stitch until Back measures approximately {4½-5-5½}{6-6½-7}"/ {11.5-12.5-14}{15-16.5-18} cm from markers, ending by working a **purl** row; cut yarn.

Slip all sts onto a circular needle; place point protectors on needle. The Back will be joined to the Fronts at the shoulders using 3-needle bind off.

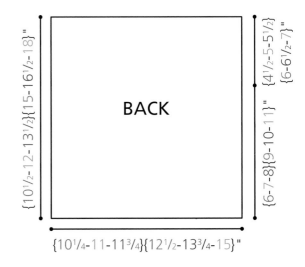

BACK

{10½-12-13½}{15-16½-18}"

{4½-5-5½}{6-6½-7}"

{6-7-8}{9-10-11}"

{10¼-11-11¾}{12½-13¾-15}"

LEFT FRONT

Using straight needles and Main Color, cast on {25-27-29}{31-35-37} sts.

Work same as Back until Front measures approximately {6-7-8}{9-10-11}"/{15-18-20.5}{23-25.5-28} cm from cast on edge.

Note: Place a marker around stitch at side edge to indicate Sleeve placement.

Work even until Front measures approximately {8½-10-11½}{13-14½-16}"/{21.5-25.5-29}{33-37-40.5} cm from cast on edge, ending by working a **knit** row.

CREWNECK SHAPING

Row 1: Bind off {5-6-7}{7-9-8} sts, work across: {20-21-22}{24-26-29} sts.

Row 2: Work across.

Row 3 (Decrease row): Bind off 2 sts, work across: {18-19-20}{22-24-27} sts.

Rows 4-7: Repeat Rows 2 and 3 twice: {14-15-16}{18-20-23} sts.

Work even until Front measures same as Back, ending by working a **purl** row; do **not** cut yarn.

With **right** sides together and Back in front of Front, work 3-needle bind off to join the Left Front and Back shoulders *(Fig. 12, page 125)*.

RIGHT FRONT

Work same as Left Front to Crewneck Shaping, ending by working a **purl** row; then work Crewneck Shaping same as Left Front.

Slip {14-15-16}{18-20-23} right shoulder sts from Back neck circular needle onto a straight needle, leaving remaining {23-25-27}{27-29-29} neck sts on circular needle. Using a double pointed needle, work 3-needle bind off to join the Right Front and Back shoulders.

BOXY SLEEVE

With **right** side of Body facing, using straight needles and Main Color, pick up {45-51-55}{61-65-71} sts evenly spaced between markers *(Fig. 11a, page 125)*; remove markers.

Beginning with a **purl** row, work in Stockinette Stitch until Sleeve measures approximately {4-5-6}{8-10-12}"/{10-12.5-15}{20.5-25.5-30.5} cm or ¾" (2 cm) less than desired length, ending by working a **purl** row.

Knit 6 rows for Garter Stitch Edging.

Bind off all sts in **knit**.

Repeat for second Boxy Sleeve.

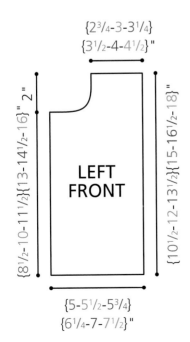

{2¾-3-3¼}
{3½-4-4½}"

2"

{8½-10-11½}{13-14½-16}"

LEFT FRONT

{10½-12-13½}{15-16½-18}"

{5-5½-5¾}
{6¼-7-7½}"

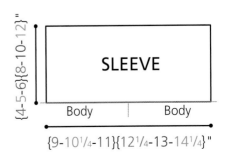

{4-5-6}{8-10-12}"

SLEEVE

Body | Body

{9-10¼-11}{12¼-13-14¼}"

HEART APPLIQUÉ

Using straight needles and Contrasting Color, cast on 15 sts, place marker, cast on 15 sts: 30 sts.

Row 1 (Right side): Knit increase, knit across to within 2 sts of marker, SSK, K2 tog, knit across to last st, knit increase.

Row 2: Knit across.

Rows 3-12: Repeat Rows 1 and 2, 5 times: 6 ridges.

Row 13 (Decrease row): Knit across to within 2 sts of marker, SSK, K2 tog, knit across: 28 sts.

Row 14: Knit across.

Rows 15 and 16: Repeat Rows 13 and 14: 26 sts.

Row 17 (Decrease row): SSK, knit across to within 2 sts of marker, SSK, K2 tog, knit across to last 2 sts, K2 tog: 22 sts.

Row 18: Knit across.

Rows 19 and 20: Repeat Rows 17 and 18: 18 sts.

Bind off remaining sts in knit leaving a long end for sewing.

Pin appliqué to Left Front, then sew in place.

FINISHING

Weave underarm and side in one continuous seam, one half stitch in (Fig. 13, page 125).

GARTER STITCH FRONT BAND

With right side facing, using straight needles and Main Color, pick up {41-49-57}{65-71-79} sts evenly spaced along one Front edge.

Knit 7 rows.

Bind off all sts in knit.

Repeat for second Front.

HOOD

With right side facing, using circular needle (holding Back neck sts) and Main Color, pick up 4 sts across Right Front Band and {5-6-7}{7-9-8} sts across bound off sts (Fig. 11b, page 125), pick up 10 sts evenly spaced along neck edge, knit {11-12-13}{13-14-14} sts across Back neck, place marker, knit across remaining {12-13-14}{14-15-15} Back neck sts, pick up 10 sts evenly spaced along Left Front neck edge, pick up {5-6-7}{7-9-8} sts across bound off sts and 4 sts across Front Band: {61-65-69}{69-75-73} sts.

Row 1: K5, purl across to last 5 sts, K5.

Row 2 (Increase row): Knit across to marker, M1, slip marker, K1, M1, knit across: {63-67-71}{71-77-75} sts.

Rows 3-20: Repeat Rows 1 and 2, 9 times: {81-85-89}{89-95-93} sts.

Work even until Hood measures approximately {8-8-8}{9-9-9}"/{20.5-20.5-20.5}{23-23-23} cm **or** to desired length.

Slide the sts to the center of the cable. Fold the cable in half with **right** sides together and pull it between the center sts forming a loop *(Fig. 1, page 111)*: {40-42-44}{44-47-47} sts on one side.

Work 3-needle bind off to join top of Hood, working last 3 sts together.

Block cardigan *(see Blocking, page 126)*.

ZIPPER

Pin zipper in place carefully aligning bottom edge of zipper with edging of sweater. If zipper is too long for Front, open zipper, cut zipper length from the top, stitch a heavy zipper stop with thread and fold excess zipper to wrong side. Hand sew zipper in place.

Hooded Sweat Shirt

◖■■◻◻ EASY +

FEATURED DETAILS

- Rolled Edging
- Stockinette Stitch fabric
- Crewneck Pullover
- Long Sleeves
- Pullover Kangaroo Pocket
- Hood

SHOPPING LIST

Yarn (Medium Weight) 🧶 4

[3.5 ounces, 220 yards
(100 grams, 201 meters) per ball]:
☐ {2-3-3}{3-4-4} balls

Knitting Needles

☐ Straight needles, size 6 (4 mm)
☐ Double pointed needles, size 6 (4 mm)
☐ 24-36" (61-91.5 cm) circular needle, size 6 (4 mm)
  or sizes needed for gauge

Additional Supplies

☐ Point protectors for circular needle
☐ Stitch holder
☐ Markers - split ring, locked, or scrap yarn
☐ Yarn needle
☐ Pins

SIZE INFORMATION

Sizes	Finished Chest Measurement	
6 months	20"	(51 cm)
12 months	21¹/₂"	(54.5 cm)
18 months	23¹/₄"	(59 cm)
2 years	24³/₄"	(63 cm)
4 years	27¹/₄"	(69 cm)
6 years	29¹/₂"	(75 cm)

Size Note: We have printed the instructions for the sizes in different colors to make it easier for you to find:

- 6 months in Purple
- 12 months in Lt Blue
- 18 months in Pink
- 2 years in Orange
- 4 years in Blue
- 6 years in Green

Instructions in black apply to all sizes.

GAUGE INFORMATION

In Stockinette Stitch (knit one row, purl one row),
  20 sts and 28 rows = 4" (10 cm)

TECHNIQUES USED

- M1 *(Figs. 5a & b, page 123)*
- K2 tog *(Fig. 7, page 124)*
- SSK *(Figs. 8a-c, page 124)*

BACK

Using straight needles, cast on {51-55-59} {63-69-75} sts.

Note: First 10 rows form the Rolled Edge.

Beginning with a **knit** row, work in Stockinette Stitch until Back measures approximately {6-7-8} {9-10-11}"/{15-18-20.5}{23-25.5-28} cm from bottom edge (allowing the Edging to roll).

Note: Place a marker around the first and last stitch to indicate Sleeve placement *(see Markers, page 121).*

Continue working in Stockinette Stitch until Back measures approximately {4½-5-5½}{6-6½-7}"/ {11.5-12.5-14}{15-16.5-18} cm from markers, ending by working a **purl** row; cut yarn.

Slip all sts onto a circular needle; place point protectors on needle. The Back will be joined to the Front at the shoulders using 3-needle bind off.

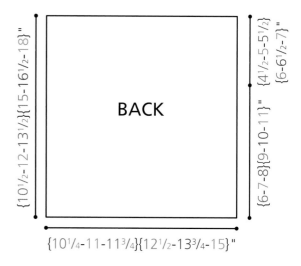

{10½-12-13½}{15-16½-18}"

{4½-5-5½} {6-6½-7}"/

BACK

{6-7-8}{9-10-11}"

{10¼-11-11¾}{12½-13¾-15}"

FRONT

Work same as Back until Front measures approximately {8½-10-11½}{13-14½-16}"/ {21.5-25.5-29}{33-37-40.5} cm from bottom edge (allowing the Edging to roll), ending by working a **purl** row: {51-55-59}{63-69-75} sts.

CREWNECK SHAPING

Both sides of Neck are worked at the same time using separate yarn for each side.

Row 1: Knit {20-21-22}{24-26-29} sts; with second yarn, knit across center {11-13-15}{15-17-17} sts and slip these sts onto a st holder; knit across: {20-21-22}{24-26-29} sts **each** side.

Rows 2-7: Work across first side; with second yarn, bind off 2 sts, work across: {14-15-16} {18-20-23} sts **each** side.

Work even until Front measures same as Back, ending by working a **purl** row; do **not** cut yarn.

With **right** sides together and Back in front of Front, work 3-needle bind off to join the left Front and Back shoulders *(Fig. 12, page 125)*.

Slip {14-15-16}{18-20-23} right shoulder sts from Back neck circular needle onto a straight needle, leaving remaining {23-25-27}{27-29-29} neck sts on circular needle. Using a double pointed needle, work 3-needle bind off to join the right Front and Back shoulders.

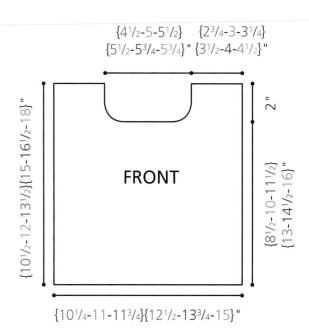

{4½-5-5½} {2¾-3-3¼}
{5½-5¾-5¾}" {3½-4-4½}"

2"

{10½-12-13½}{15-16½-18}"

FRONT

{8½-10-11½}
{13-14½-16}"

{10¼-11-11¾}{12½-13¾-15}"

LONG SLEEVE

With **right** side of Body facing and using straight needles, pick up {45-51-55}{61-65-71} sts evenly spaced between markers *(Fig. 11a, page 125)*; remove markers.

Row 1: Purl across.

Row 2: Knit across.

Row 3: Purl across.

Row 4 (Decrease row): K1, K2 tog, knit across to last 3 sts, SSK, K1: {43-49-53}{59-63-69} sts.

Repeat Rows 1-4, {9-11-11}{13-14-16} times: {25-27-31}{33-35-37} sts.

Work even until Sleeve measures approximately {6-7-8}{10-12-14}"/{15-18-20.5} {25.5-30.5-35.5} cm **or** ¹/₂" (1.5 cm) less than desired length, ending by working a **purl** row.

Work in Stockinette Stitch for an additional 10 rows for a Rolled Edge.

Bind off all sts **loosely** in **knit**.

KANGAROO POCKET

Using straight needles, cast on {41-41-41} {51-51-51} sts.

Beginning with a **purl** row, work in Stockinette Stitch for {1-1-1¹/₂}{2-2-2}"/{2.5-2.5-4}{5-5-5} cm, ending by working a **purl** row.

SHAPING

Row 1 (Decrease row): K5, K2 tog, knit across to last 7 sts, SSK, K5: {39-39-39}{49-49-49} sts.

Row 2: K5, purl across to last 5 sts, K5.

Repeat Rows 1 and 2, {9-9-9}{12-12-12} times: {21-21-21}{25-25-25} sts.

Bind off remaining sts in **knit** leaving a long for sewing.

Using photo as a guide for placement, page 65, pin Pocket to Front, then sew in place along top, bottom, and straight side edges.

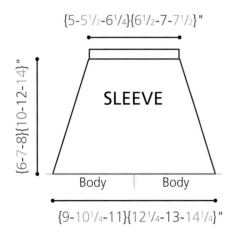

{5-5¹/₂-6¹/₄}{6¹/₂-7-7¹/₂}"

{6-7-8}{10-12-14}"

SLEEVE

Body | Body

{9-10¹/₄-11}{12¹/₄-13-14¹/₄}"

FINISHING

Weave underarm and side in one continuous seam, one half stitch in *(Fig. 13, page 125)*.

HOOD

With **right** side facing, slip {5-6-7}{7-8-8} sts from Front neck st holder onto circular needle (holding Back neck sts), bind off next st (center), knit across remaining {4-5-6}{6-7-7} sts on st holder, pick up 10 sts evenly spaced along right Front neck edge *(Fig. 11b, page 125)*, knit {11-12-13}{13-14-14} sts across Back neck, place marker, knit across remaining {12-13-14}{14-15-15} Back neck sts, pick up 10 sts evenly spaced along left Front neck edge, knit across to bound off st: {53-57-61}{61-65-65} sts.

Row 1 (Wrong side): K5, purl across to last 5 sts, K5.

Row 2 (Increase row): Knit across to marker, M1, slip marker, K1, M1, knit across: {55-59-63}{63-67-67} sts.

Rows 3-20: Repeat Rows 1 and 2, 9 times: {73-77-81}{81-85-85} sts.

Work even until Hood measures approximately {8-8-8}{9-9-9}"/{20.5-20.5-20.5}{23-23-23} cm **or** to desired length.

Slide the sts to the center of the cable. Fold the cable in half with **right** sides together and pull it between the center sts forming a loop *(Fig. 1, page 111)*: {36-38-40}{40-42-42} sts on one side.

Work 3-needle bind off to join top of Hood, working last 3 sts together.

65

Snapped V-Neck Cardi

■■□□ EASY +

FEATURED DETAILS

- Ribbing Edging
- Stockinette Stitch fabric
- V-Neck Cardigan
- Long Sleeves
- Cardigan Kangaroo Pocket
- Ribbing Band
- Snap closure

SHOPPING LIST

Yarn (Medium Weight) **[4]** MEDIUM
[3.5 ounces, 220 yards
(100 grams, 201 meters) per ball]:
- ☐ {2-2-2}{2-3-3} balls

Knitting Needles
- ☐ Straight needles, size 6 (4 mm)
- ☐ Double pointed needles, size 6 (4 mm)
- ☐ 24-36" (61-91.5 cm) circular needle, size 6 (4 mm)
  or sizes needed for gauge

Additional Supplies
- ☐ Point protectors for circular needle
- ☐ Markers - split ring, locked, or scrap yarn
- ☐ Yarn needle
- ☐ Sewing needle and thread
- ☐ ³/₈" (10 mm) Snaps - {4-4-5}{5-6-6}
- ☐ Snap attaching tool
- ☐ ⁵/₈" (16 mm) Grosgrain ribbon - {14-16-18} {20-22-24}"/{35.5-40.5-45.5} {51-56-61} cm
- ☐ Pins

SIZE INFORMATION

Sizes	Finished Chest Measurement	
6 months	20³/₄"	(52.5 cm)
12 months	22¹/₂"	(57 cm)
18 months	24"	(61 cm)
2 years	25¹/₂"	(65 cm)
4 years	28¹/₂"	(72.5 cm)
6 years	30¹/₂"	(77.5 cm)

Size Note: We have printed the instructions for the sizes in different colors to make it easier for you to find:
- 6 months in Purple
- 12 months in Lt Blue
- 18 months in Pink
- 2 years in Orange
- 4 years in Blue
- 6 years in Green

Instructions in black apply to all sizes.

GAUGE INFORMATION

In Stockinette Stitch (knit one row, purl one row),
  20 sts and 28 rows = 4" (10 cm)

TECHNIQUES USED

- K2 tog *(Fig. 7, page 124)*
- SSK *(Figs. 8a-c, page 124)*

BACK
RIBBING
Using straight needles, cast on {51-55-59} {63-69-75} sts.

Row 1 (Right side): K1, (P1, K1) across.

Row 2: P1, (K1, P1) across.

Rows 3-6: Repeat Rows 1 and 2 twice.

BODY
Beginning with a **knit** row, work in Stockinette Stitch until Back measures approximately {6-7-8}{9-10-11}"/{15-18-20.5}{23-25.5-28} cm from cast on edge.

Note: Place a marker around the first and last stitch to indicate Sleeve placement (see Markers, page 121).

Continue working in Stockinette Stitch until Back measures approximately {4½-5-5½}{6-6½-7}"/ {11.5-12.5-14}{15-16.5-18} cm from markers, ending by working a **purl** row; cut yarn.

Slip all sts onto a circular needle; place point protectors on needle. The Back will be joined to the Fronts at the shoulders using 3-needle bind off.

LEFT FRONT
RIBBING
Using straight needles, cast on {25-27-29} {31-35-37} sts.

Row 1 (Right side): K1, (P1, K1) across.

Row 2: P1, (K1, P1) across.

Rows 3-6: Repeat Rows 1 and 2 twice.

BODY
Beginning with a **knit** row, work in Stockinette Stitch until Front measures approximately {6-7-8} {9-10-11}"/{15-18-20.5}{23-25.5-28} cm from cast on edge, ending by working a **purl** row.

Note: Place a marker around the first and last stitch to indicate Sleeve and Neck Band placement.

V-NECK SHAPING
Sizes 6, 12, & 18 Months ONLY
Row 1 (Decrease row): Knit across to last 3 sts, SSK, K1: {24-26-28} sts.

Row 2: Purl across.

Repeat Rows 1 and 2, {10-11-12} times: {14-15-16} sts.

Sizes 2, 4, & 6 ONLY
Row 1 (Decrease row): Knit across to last 3 sts, SSK, K1: {30-34-36} sts.

Row 2: Purl across.

Row 3 (Decrease row): Knit across to last 3 sts, SSK, K1: {29-33-35} sts.

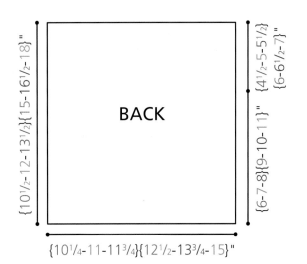

{10½-12-13½}{15-16½-18}"

{4½-5-5½}{6-6½-7}"

{6-7-8}{9-10-11}"

BACK

{10¼-11-11¾}{12½-13¾-15}"

Rows 4-6: Work across.

Repeat Rows 1-6, {5-6-6} times; then repeat Row 1, {1-1-0} time(s) **more** *(see Zeros, page 121)*: {18-20-23} sts.

All Sizes
Work even until Front measures same as Back, ending by working a **purl** row; do **not** cut yarn.

With **right** sides together and Back in front of Front, work 3-needle bind off to join the Left Front and Back shoulders *(Fig. 12, page 125)*.

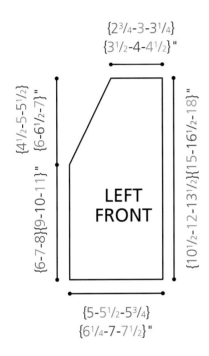

{2³/₄-3-3¹/₄}
{3¹/₂-4-4¹/₂}"

{4¹/₂-5-5¹/₂}
{6-6¹/₂-7}"

{6-7-8}{9-10-11}"

LEFT FRONT

{10¹/₂-12-13¹/₂}{15-16¹/₂-18}"

{5-5¹/₂-5³/₄}
{6¹/₄-7-7¹/₂}"

RIGHT FRONT
Work same as Left Front to V-Neck Shaping: {25-27-29}{31-35-37} sts.

Note: Place a marker around the first and last stitch to indicate Sleeve and Ribbing Band placement.

V-NECK SHAPING
Sizes 6, 12, & 18 Months ONLY
Row 1 (Decrease row): K1, K2 tog, knit across: {24-26-28} sts.

Row 2: Purl across.

Repeat Rows 1 and 2, {10-11-12} times: {14-15-16} sts.

Sizes 2, 4, & 6 ONLY
Row 1 (Decrease row): K1, K2 tog, knit across: {30-34-36} sts.

Row 2: Purl across.

Row 3 (Decrease row): K1, K2 tog, knit across: {29-33-35} sts.

Rows 4-6: Work across.

Repeat Rows 1-6, {5-6-6} times; then repeat Row 1, {1-1-0} time(s) **more**: {18-20-23} sts.

All Sizes
Work even until Front measures same as Back, ending by working a **purl** row; do **not** cut yarn.

Slip {14-15-16}{18-20-23} right shoulder sts from Back neck circular needle onto a straight needle, leaving remaining {23-25-27}{27-29-29} neck sts on circular needle. Using a double pointed needle, work 3-needle bind off to join the Right Front and Back shoulders.

LONG SLEEVE

With **right** side of Body facing and using straight needles, pick up {45-51-55}{61-65-71} sts evenly spaced between markers *(Fig. 11a, page 125)*; remove markers.

Row 1: Purl across.

Row 2: Knit across.

Row 3: Purl across.

Row 4 (Decrease row): K1, K2 tog, knit across to last 3 sts, SSK, K1: {43-49-53}{59-63-69} sts.

Repeat Rows 1-4, {9-11-11}{13-14-16} times: {25-27-31}{33-35-37} sts.

Work even until Sleeve measures approximately {6-7-8}{10-12-14}"/{15-18-20.5} {25.5-30.5-35.5} cm **or** 1¼" (3 cm) less than desired length, ending by working a **purl** row.

RIBBING
Row 1: K1, (P1, K1) across.

Row 2: P1, (K1, P1) across.

Rows 3-6: Repeat Rows 1 and 2 twice.

Bind off all sts **loosely** in pattern.

Repeat for second Long Sleeve.

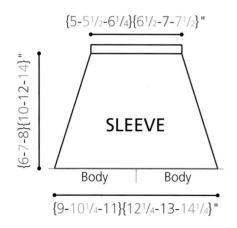

{5-5½-6¼}{6½-7-7½}"

{6-7-8}{10-12-14}"

SLEEVE

Body | Body

{9-10¼-11}{12¼-13-14¼}"

KANGAROO POCKETS
LEFT FRONT POCKET

Using straight needles, cast on {20-20-20} {25-25-25} sts.

Beginning with a **purl** row, work in Stockinette Stitch for {1-1-1½}{2-2-2}"/{2.5-2.5-4}{5-5-5} cm, ending by working a **purl** row.

SHAPING
Row 1 (Decrease row): K5, K2 tog, knit across: {19-19-19}{24-24-24} sts.

Row 2: Purl across to last 5 sts, K5.

Repeat Rows 1 and 2, {9-9-9}{12-12-12} times: {10-10-10}{12-12-12} sts.

Bind off remaining sts in **knit**.

Using photo as a guide for placement, page 71, pin Pocket to Left Front placing long vertical edge one stitch in from front edge, then sew in place along top, bottom, and straight side edges.

RIGHT FRONT POCKET

Using straight needles, cast on {20-20-20} {25-25-25} sts.

Beginning with a **purl** row, work in Stockinette Stitch for {1-1-1½}{2-2-2}"/{2.5-2.5-4}{5-5-5} cm, ending by working a **purl** row.

SHAPING
Row 1 (Decrease row): Knit across to last 7 sts, SSK, K5: {19-19-19}{24-24-24} sts.

Row 2: K5, purl across.

Repeat Rows 1 and 2, {9-9-9}{12-12-12} times: {10-10-10}{12-12-12} sts.

Bind off remaining sts in **knit**.

Using Left Front as a guide for placement, pin Pocket to Right Front placing long vertical edge one stitch in from front edge, then sew in place along top, bottom, and straight side edges.

FINISHING
Weave underarm and side in one continuous seam, one half stitch in *(Fig. 13, page 125)*.

RIBBING BAND
With **right** side facing, using circular needle (holding Back neck sts), and beginning at Right Front Edging, pick up {29-35-41}{47-53-55} sts evenly spaced across to marker, remove marker, pick up {22-24-26}{28-30-32} sts evenly spaced across neck edge to shoulder, knit {23-25-27}{27-29-29} sts across Back neck, pick up {22-24-26}{28-30-32} sts evenly spaced across Left Front neck edge to marker, remove marker, pick up {29-35-41}{47-53-55} sts evenly spaced across: {125-143-161}{177-195-203} sts.

Row 1: K1, (P1, K1) across.

Row 2: P1, (K1, P1) across.

Rows 3-7: Repeat Rows 1 and 2 twice, then repeat Row 1 once **more**.

Bind off all sts in pattern.

Block cardigan *(see Blocking, page 126)*.

SNAP CLOSURE
Cut 2 pieces of grosgrain ribbon, each 1 " (2.5 cm) longer than Front from bottom edge to V-Neck shaping. Fold ends under ½" (1.25 cm). Hand sew ribbon to **wrong** side of each Front along Front Band.

Attach snaps through knitting and ribbon, keeping in mind that a Girl's cardigan Front laps right over left and a Boy's cardigan laps left over right.

Striped Crewneck Cardi

◼◼◻◻ EASY +

FEATURED DETAILS

- Garter Stitch Edging
- Striped (Stockinette Stitch) fabric
- Crewneck Cardigan
- Long Sleeves
- Side Seam Pockets
- Garter Stitch Front and Neck Band
- Button closure

SHOPPING LIST

Yarn (Medium Weight)
[6 ounces, 315 yards
(170 grams, 288 meters) per skein]:
☐ Main Color (Purple) - {1-1-1}{1-1-2} skein(s)
☐ Contrasting Color (Green) - {1-1-1}{1-1-2} skein(s)

Knitting Needles
☐ Straight needles, size 6 (4 mm)
☐ Double pointed needles, size 6 (4 mm)
☐ 24-36" (61-91.5 cm) circular needle, size 6 (4 mm)
or sizes needed for gauge

Additional Supplies
☐ Point protectors for circular needle
☐ Markers - split ring, locked, or scrap yarn
☐ Yarn needle
☐ Sewing needle and thread
☐ ¾ " (19 mm) Buttons - {4-4-5}{5-6-6}
☐ Pins

SIZE INFORMATION

Sizes	Finished Chest Measurement	
6 months	20½"	(52 cm)
12 months	22¼"	(56.5 cm)
18 months	23¾"	(60.5 cm)
2 years	25¼"	(64 cm)
4 years	28¼"	(72 cm)
6 years	30¼"	(77 cm)

Size Note: We have printed the instructions for the sizes in different colors to make it easier for you to find:
- 6 months in Purple
- 12 months in Lt Blue
- 18 months in Pink
- 2 years in Orange
- 4 years in Blue
- 6 years in Green

Instructions in black apply to all sizes.

GAUGE INFORMATION

In Stockinette Stitch (knit one row, purl one row),
20 sts and 28 rows = 4" (10 cm)

TECHNIQUES USED

- YO *(Fig. 3a, page 122)*
- K2 tog *(Fig. 7, page 124)*
- SSK *(Figs. 8a-c, page 124)*

BACK
GARTER STITCH EDGING
Using straight needles and Main Color, cast on {51-55-59}{63-69-75} sts.

Knit 6 rows.

BODY
Stripe Sequence: ★ 6 Rows of Contrasting Color, 6 rows of Main Color; repeat from ★ for stripe sequence.

Note: Carry unused color loosely along the side edge, twisting colors every 2 rows to prevent long strands along the edge.

Working in stripe sequence and beginning with a **knit** row, work in Stockinette Stitch until Back measures approximately {6-7-8}{9-10-11}"/ {15-18-20.5}{23-25.5-28} cm from cast on edge.

Note: Place a marker around the first and last stitch to indicate Sleeve placement *(see Markers, page 121).*

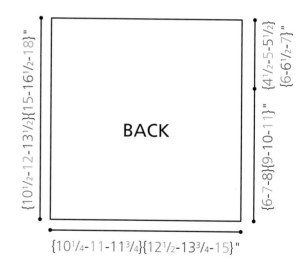

{10½-12-13½}{15-16½-18}" {4½-5-5½}{6-6½-7}"

BACK

{6-7-8}{9-10-11}"

{10¼-11-11¾}{12½-13¾-15}"

Continue working in Stockinette Stitch until Back measures approximately {4½-5-5½}{6-6½-7}"/ {11.5-12.5-14}{15-16.5-18} cm from markers, ending by working a **purl** row; cut yarn.

Slip all sts onto a circular needle; place point protectors on needle. The Back will be joined to the Fronts at the shoulders using 3-needle bind off.

LEFT FRONT
GARTER STITCH EDGING
Using straight needles and Main Color, cast on {25-27-29}{31-35-37} sts.

Knit 6 rows.

BODY
Working in stripe sequence and beginning with a **knit** row, work in Stockinette Stitch until Front measures approximately {6-7-8}{9-10-11}"/ {15-18-20.5}{23-25.5-28} cm from cast on edge.

Note: Place a marker around stitch at side edge to indicate Sleeve placement.

Work even until Front measures approximately {8½-10-11½}{13-14½-16}"/{21.5-25.5-29} {33-37-40.5} cm from cast on edge, ending by working a **knit** row.

CREWNECK SHAPING
Row 1: Bind off {5-6-7}{7-9-8} sts, work across: {20-21-22}{24-26-29} sts.

Row 2: Work across.

Row 3 (Decrease row): Bind off 2 sts, work across: {18-19-20}{22-24-27} sts.

Rows 4-7: Repeat Rows 2 and 3 twice: {14-15-16} {18-20-23} sts.

Work even until Front measures same as Back, ending by working a **purl** row; do **not** cut yarn.

With **right** sides together and Back in front of Front, work 3-needle bind off to join the Left Front and Back shoulders *(Fig. 12, page 125)*.

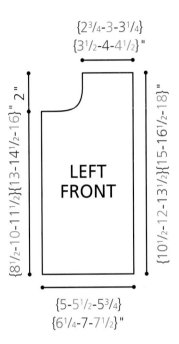

{2¾-3-3¼}
{3½-4-4½}"

2"

{8½-10-11½}{13-14½-16}"

LEFT FRONT

{10½-12-13½}{15-16½-18}"

{5-5½-5¾}
{6¼-7-7½}"

RIGHT FRONT
Work same as Left Front to Crewneck Shaping, ending by working a **purl** row; then work Crewneck Shaping same as Left Front.

Slip {14-15-16}{18-20-23} right shoulder sts from Back neck circular needle onto a straight needle, leaving remaining {23-25-27}{27-29-29} neck sts on circular needle. Using a double pointed needle, work 3-needle bind off to join the Right Front and Back shoulders.

LONG SLEEVE

With **right** side of Body facing, using straight needles and Contrasting Color, pick up {45-51-55}{61-65-71} sts evenly spaced between markers *(Fig. 11a, page 125)*; remove markers.

Stripe Sequence: ★ 6 Rows of Contrasting Color, 6 rows of Main Color; repeat from ★ for stripe sequence.

Row 1: Purl across.

Row 2: Knit across.

Row 3: Purl across.

Row 4 (Decrease row): K1, K2 tog, knit across to last 3 sts, SSK, K1: {43-49-53}{59-63-69} sts.

Repeat Rows 1-4, {9-11-11}{13-14-16} times: {25-27-31}{33-35-37} sts.

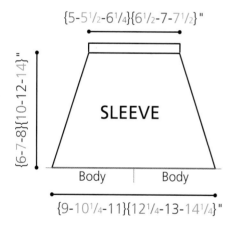

{5-5½-6¼}{6½-7-7½}"

{6-7-8}{10-12-14}"

SLEEVE

Body | Body

{9-10¼-11}{12¼-13-14¼}"

Work even until Sleeve measures approximately {6-7-8}{10-12-14}"/{15-18-20.5}{25.5-30.5-35.5} cm or ¾" (2 cm) less than desired length, ending by working a **purl** row.

Cut Contrasting Color.

Using Main Color, knit 6 rows for Garter Stitch Edging.

Bind off all sts **loosely** in **knit**.

Repeat for second Long Sleeve.

SIDE SEAM POCKET (Make 2)

Using straight needles and Main Color, and leaving a long end for sewing, cast on {30-32-34}{36-38-40} sts.

Beginning with a **purl** row, work in Stockinette Stitch until Pocket measures approximately {3-3-3½}{3½-4-4}"/{7.5-7.5-9}{9-10-10} cm from cast on edge.

Bind off all sts leaving a long end for sewing.

Fold Pocket in half widthwise, with **right** side together. Sew across top and bottom edges.

Pin Pocket to **wrong** side of Front and Back placing bottom edge above the bottom Edging.

FINISHING

Beginning at bottom edge, weave side of Front and Back together along Edging, one half stitch in *(Fig. 13, page 125)*, then weave one side of Pocket in place. Weave remaining side of Pocket in place, then weave remaining side and underarm in one continuous seam.

Buttonhole Band is made on Right Front for Girl's Sweater and on Left Front for Boy's Sweater.

GARTER STITCH BUTTONHOLE BAND

With **right** side facing, using straight needles and Main Color, pick up {41-49-57}{65-71-79} sts evenly spaced along one Front edge.

Rows 1-3: Knit across.

Place markers for buttonholes, placing a marker ³/₄" (2 cm) above cast on edge and ¹/₂" (1.25 cm) from top edge, then evenly spacing markers for remaining {2-2-3}{3-4-4} buttonholes.

Row 4 (Buttonhole row): ★ Knit across to marker, YO, K2 tog; repeat from ★ {3-3-4}{4-5-5} times **more**, knit across.

Rows 5-7: Knit across.

Bind off all sts **loosely** in **knit**.

GARTER STITCH BUTTON BAND

With **right** side facing, using straight needles and Main Color, pick up {41-49-57}{65-71-79} sts evenly spaced along opposite Front edge.

Knit 7 rows.

Bind off all sts in **knit**.

Sew {4-4-5}{5-6-6} buttons to Front Band to correspond with buttonholes.

GARTER STITCH NECK BAND

With **right** side facing, using circular needle (holding Back neck sts) and Main Color, pick up 4 sts across Right Front Band and {5-6-7}{7-9-8} sts across bound off sts *(Fig. 11b, page 125)*, pick up 10 sts evenly spaced along neck edge, knit {23-25-27}{27-29-29} sts across Back neck, pick up 10 sts evenly spaced along Left Front neck edge, pick up {5-6-7}{7-9-8} sts across bound off sts and 4 sts across Front Band: {61-65-69} {69-75-73} sts.

Knit 5 rows.

Bind off all sts in **knit**.

Picking the Pieces

Plan your customized sweater by choosing from 48 options for the edging, fabric, front, sleeves, pockets, appliqués, and finishing for pullovers or cardigans.

Easy knit sweaters

All of the sweaters in this book are drop shoulder, which means that the body is knit straight from the cast on edge to the shoulder, with no shaping at all. It is easy to knit and is also comfortable for children because there is a lot of room for movement. This style even looks good slightly large and allows for growing room.

Envision your customized sweater

Look through the different options in each chapter. A fun way to envision your customized sweater is to photocopy or trace the shapes on pages 80-82; then cut them out. Arrange them as you would puzzle pieces, changing the sleeves or the front closure until you are pleased with the combination, as illustrated on page 83. The pieces can be kept in an envelope, so they will be handy in creating your next sweater. Or just make a list of each of the options you choose. Remember, the possible combinations are almost endless!

Or plan as you go

Your sweater doesn't have to be pre-planned. If you like, just pick one option at a time and see your creation develop as-you-go. Begin with chapter 1, page 85; then follow the chapters in order.

Be creative!

You can knit the bottom edgings, neckline band, or the pockets in a different color from the body of the sweater. Because all of the pieces are interchangeable, the sleeves can be knit in a different fabric from the body, or a different edging can be used. Mix and match necklines, pockets, and appliqués — it's all your choice!

Fronts

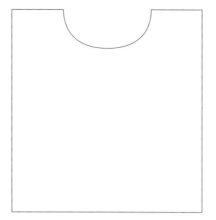

Crewneck Pullover pg. 92

V-Neck Pullover pg. 93

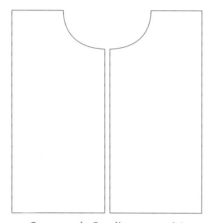

Crewneck Cardigan pg. 94

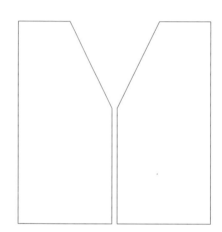

V-Neck Cardigan pg. 95

Edging

Note: All Edgings can be placed on Pullovers and Cardigans.

Garter Stitch pg. 86

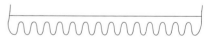

Picots pg. 87

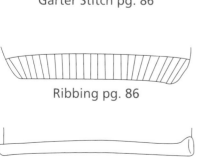

Ribbing pg. 86

Ruffle pg. 87

Rolled Edge pg. 87

Lace pg. 88

Sleeves

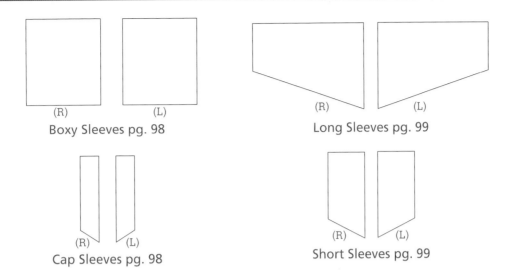

(R) (L)
Boxy Sleeves pg. 98

(R) (L)
Long Sleeves pg. 99

(R) (L)
Cap Sleeves pg. 98

(R) (L)
Short Sleeves pg. 99

Pockets

Note: The Patch Pockets and Side Seam Pockets can be placed on Pullovers and Cardigans

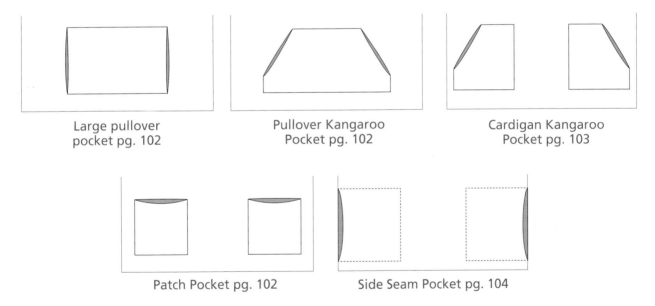

Large pullover
pocket pg. 102

Pullover Kangaroo
Pocket pg. 102

Cardigan Kangaroo
Pocket pg. 103

Patch Pocket pg. 102

Side Seam Pocket pg. 104

Appliqués

pg. 106 pg. 106 pg. 107 pg. 107 pg. 108

Pullover Finishing

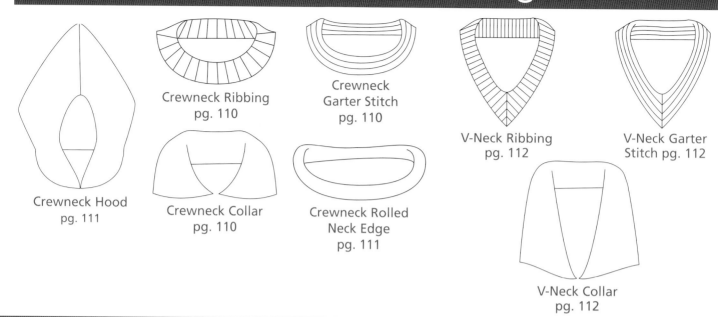

Crewneck Hood
pg. 111

Crewneck Ribbing
pg. 110

Crewneck Collar
pg. 110

Crewneck Garter Stitch
pg. 110

Crewneck Rolled Neck Edge
pg. 111

V-Neck Ribbing
pg. 112

V-Neck Garter Stitch pg. 112

V-Neck Collar
pg. 112

Cardigan Finishing

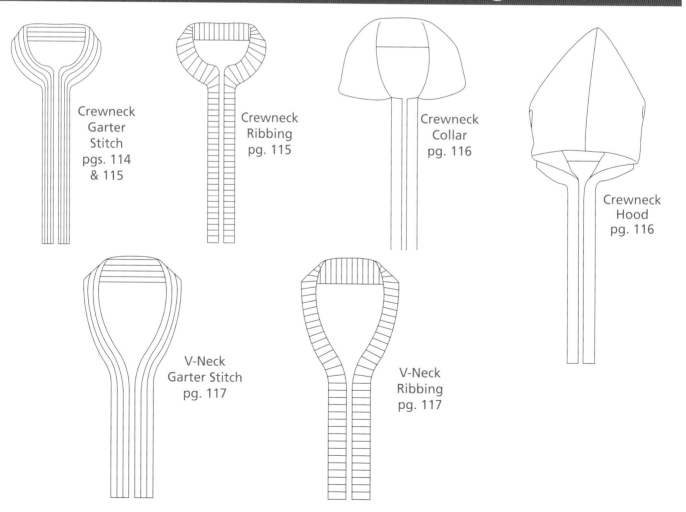

Crewneck Garter Stitch
pgs. 114 & 115

Crewneck Ribbing
pg. 115

Crewneck Collar
pg. 116

Crewneck Hood
pg. 116

V-Neck Garter Stitch
pg. 117

V-Neck Ribbing
pg. 117

Mix and Match!

Photocopy or trace the shapes on pages 80-82; then cut them out and arrange them into your customized sweater. You can even color them for a visual effect.

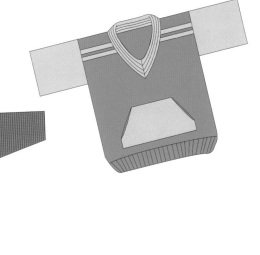

Choose a size
The sweaters are designed to have ease, allowing garments to be worn under them and also for the child to be able to move easily. The measurements given are the finished chest measurements of the sweaters, which vary slightly depending on the sweater style. When choosing what size to make, you may want to measure your child's favorite sweater that has similar styling and knit the size with the nearest finished measurement. Don't hesitate to make the body and sleeves a little longer; the Sleeves can always be rolled up until the child grows!

SIZE INFORMATION We have printed the instructions for the sizes in different colors to make it easier for you to find. Instructions in black apply to all sizes.

Sizes	Finished Chest Measurements				
	Pullovers	Cardigans			
		Garter (button/snaps)	Ribbing (button/snaps)	Garter (zipper/tie)	Ribbing (zipper/tie)
6 months	20" (51cm)	20½" (52 cm)	20¾" (52.5 cm)	21¼" (54 cm)	21¾" (55 cm)
12 months	21½" (54.4 cm)	22¼" (56.5 cm)	22½" (57 cm)	23" (58.5 cm)	23½" (59.5 cm)
18 months	23¼" (59 cm)	23¾" (60.5 cm)	24" (61cm)	24½" (62 cm)	25" (63.5 cm)
2 years	24¾" (63 cm)	25¼" (64 cm)	25½" (65 cm)	26" (66 cm)	26½" (67.5 cm)
4 years	27¼" (69 cm)	28¼" (72 cm)	28½" (72.5 cm)	29" (73.5 cm)	29½" (75 cm)
6 years	29½" (75 cm)	30¼" (77 cm)	30½" (77.5 cm)	31" (78.5 cm)	31½" (80 cm)

Shopping List

Yarn (Medium Weight)
- ☐ {220, 275, 335}{415, 510, 625} yards/ {201, 251, 306}{379, 466, 572} meters

Note: The yarn amounts given are only guides, as the amount required depends on the style and the pattern stitch you choose. Add an extra 120-175 yards (110-160 meters) when adding a hood. It's better to purchase too much yarn than not enough.

Knitting Needles
- ☐ Straight needles, size 6 (4 mm)
- ☐ Double pointed needles, size 6 (4 mm)
- ☐ 24-36" (61-91.5 cm) circular needle, size 6 (4 mm) **or** size needed for gauge

Additional Supplies
- ☐ Point protectors for circular needle
- ☐ Stitch holder
- ☐ Markers - split ring, locked, or scrap yarn
- ☐ Yarn needle
- ☐ Sewing needle and thread
- ☐ Pins

Optional Appliqué
- ☐ All - Contrasting Color yarn, small amount
- ☐ Sun - Black yarn or embroidery floss
- ☐ Cat - yarn or embroidery floss
- ☐ Truck - Black yarn

Optional Cardigan Closures
$5/8$" (16 mm) Buttons **or** $3/8$" (10 mm) snaps and attaching tool:
- ☐ Crewneck - {4-4-5}{5-6-6}
- ☐ V-neck - {3-4-4}{4-5-6}

$5/8$" (16 mm) Grosgrain ribbon:
- ☐ Crewneck - {21-24-27}{30-33-36}"/ {53.5-61-68.5}{76-84-91.5} cm
- ☐ V-neck - {14-16-18}{20-22-24}"/ {35.5-40.5-45.5}{51-56-61} cm

Note: Adjust length of ribbon if body length is adjusted.

Separating zipper:
- ☐ Crewneck cardigan - {9-10-12}{13-15-16}"/ {23-25.5-30.5}{33-38-40.5} cm
- ☐ V-neck cardigan - {6-7-8}{9-10-11}"/ {15-18-20.5}{23-25.5-28} cm

CHAPTER ONE

Edging Options

*The Back and all Fronts are worked from the bottom edge up,
beginning with the edging. The Back is made the same for all sweaters
and is made first. Choose one of the 6 options for the bottom edging.*

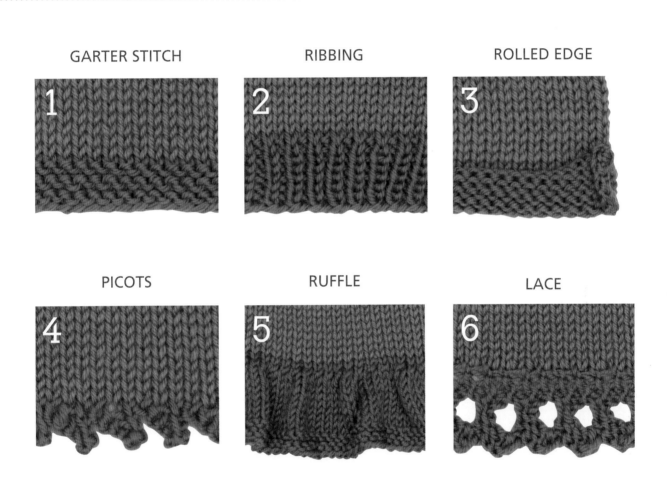

GARTER STITCH

RIBBING

ROLLED EDGE

1

2

3

PICOTS

RUFFLE

LACE

4

5

6

TIP: If you would like to see what an edging looks like on a sweater,
refer to the page(s) listed under each option's description.

GAUGE INFORMATION

Before beginning the Edging, be sure to make a gauge swatch *(see Gauge, page 121).*
In Stockinette Stitch (knit one row, purl one row),
  20 sts and 28 rows = 4" (10 cm)

1 Garter Stitch

Garter Stitch is a thick, reversible fabric that creates horizontal ridges and does not curl at the edges. It is the result of knitting every row.
(See examples on pages 7, 31, 55, and 73.)

BACK EDGING

Using straight needles, cast on {51-55-59} {63-69-75} sts.

Knit 6 rows.

2 Ribbing

Ribbing is an elastic fabric that draws in the bottom of sweaters and sleeve cuffs. It's worked on an odd number of stitches, alternating knit and purl stitches.
(See examples on pages 43, 49, and 67.)

BACK EDGING

Using straight needles, cast on {51-55-59} {63-69-75} sts.

Row 1 (Right side): K1, (P1, K1) across.

Row 2: P1, (K1, P1) across.

Rows 3-6: Repeat Rows 1 and 2 twice.

3 Rolled Edge

When Stockinette Stitch (alternating knit rows and purl rows) is worked at the bottom edge with nothing to hold it down, it rolls up, forming a fun edging.
(See examples on pages 19 and 86.)

BACK EDGING

Using straight needles, cast on {51-55-59} {63-69-75} sts.

Row 1 (Right side): Knit across.

Row 2: Purl across.

Rows 3-10: Repeat Rows 1 and 2, 4 times.

Note: When measuring the Back or Front(s) from the bottom edge, allow the Edging to roll, and measure from that point.

4 Picots

A picot edge is the perfect trim for a fabric that doesn't roll, such as Seed Stitch or Broken Rib.
(See example on page 86.)

Technique used:
• Adding new stitches *(Figs. 4a & b, page 123)*

BACK EDGING

Picot Edge: Using straight needles, place a slip knot on needle, add on 4 sts, bind off 2 sts in **knit**, slip st back onto left needle, ★ add on 5 sts, bind off 2 sts in **knit**, slip st back onto left needle; repeat from ★ until there are {51-54-57} {63-69-75} sts; add on {0-1-2}{0-0-0} st(s) *(see Zeros, page 121)*: {51-55-59}{63-69-75} sts.

5 Ruffle

This ruffle is a combination of Garter Stitch and Stockinette Stitch, and adds the right amount of frill to any girl's sweater.
(See example on page 87.)

Technique used:
• P2 tog *(Fig. 10, page 124)*

BACK EDGING

Using straight needles, cast on {102-110-118} {126-138-150} sts.

Rows 1-5: Knit across (Garter Stitch).

Row 6: Purl across.

Row 7 (Right side): Knit across.

Rows 8-11: Repeat Rows 6 and 7 twice.

Row 12: P2 tog across: {51-55-59}{63-69-75} sts.

6 Lace

This Lace is a pretty trim that can be worked in a contrasting color to add charm to any sweater. It is worked across the width of the Lace.
(See example on page 37.)

Techniques used:
• YO and YO twice *(Figs. 3a & d, page 122)*
• P2 tog *(Fig. 10, page 124)*

BACK EDGING

Using straight needles, cast on 5 sts.

When instructed to slip a stitch, always slip as if to purl.

Row 1: WYIF slip 1, K2, YO twice, P2 tog: 6 sts.

Row 2 (Right side): YO, K2, P1, K3: 7 sts.

Row 3: WYIF slip 1, K2, P4.

Row 4: WYIB and slipping first st, bind off first 2 sts, knit across: 5 sts.

Repeat Rows 1-4 until Lace measures approximately {10$\frac{1}{4}$-11-11$\frac{3}{4}$}{12$\frac{1}{2}$-13$\frac{3}{4}$-15}"/{26-28-30} {32-35-38} cm from cast on edge, ending by working Row 4.

Bind off first 3 sts in **knit** and remaining st in **purl**.

With **right** side of Lace facing, pick up {51-55-59} {63-69-75} sts evenly spaced across straight edge *(Fig. 11a, page 125)*.

What's Next?
Choose the pattern stitch that creates the fabric for the body and then complete the Back.

CHAPTER TWO
Fabric Options
Pg. 89

CHAPTER TWO

Fabric Options

*After working the Edging from Chapter 1, choose from
one of the four different pattern stitches to create your fabric.*

STOCKINETTE STITCH

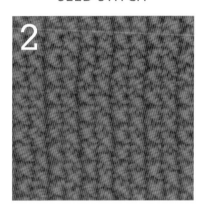

SEED STITCH

BROKEN RIB

STRIPES

Back Body

Work in chosen fabric option for pattern stitch until Back measures approximately {6-7-8}{9-10-11}"/{15-18-20.5}{23-25.5-28} cm from bottom edge.

Note: Place a marker around the first and last stitch to indicate Sleeve placement *(see Markers, page 121).*

Continue working in pattern until Back measures approximately {4½-5-5½}{6-6½-7}"/{11.5-12.5-14}{15-16.5-18} cm from markers, ending by working a **wrong** side row; cut yarn.

Slip all sts onto a circular needle; place point protectors on needle. The Back will be joined to the Front(s) at the shoulders using 3-needle bind off.

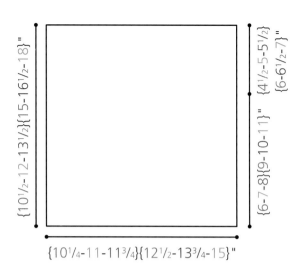

{10½-12-13½}{15-16½-18}"

{4½-5-5½}{6-6½-7}"

{6-7-8}{9-10-11}"

{10¼-11-11¾}{12½-13¾-15}"

1 Stockinette Stitch

Stockinette Stitch is the most basic stitch. Alternate knit and purl rows.
(See examples on pages 31, 37, 43, 55, 61, and 67.)

Row 1 (Right side): Knit across.

Row 2: Purl across.

Repeat Rows 1 and 2 for Stockinette Stitch.

2 Seed Stitch

Seed Stitch, also known as Moss Stitch, does not curl at the edges. Alternating knit and purl stitches, knit the purl stitches and purl the knit stitches as they face you, to form the textured pattern. The edge stitches are worked in Stockinette Stitch, making the seams easy to sew.
(See examples on pages 7, 13, and 25.)

Row 1 (Right side): K2, P1, (K1, P1) across to last 2 sts, K2.

Row 2: P1, (K1, P1) across.

Repeat Rows 1 and 2 for Seed Stitch.

3 Broken Rib

A row of knit one, purl one ribbing alternates with a row of knit stitches to form a decorative pattern.
(See example on page 19.)

Row 1 (Right side): Knit across.

Row 2: P1, (K1, P1) across.

Repeat Rows 1 and 2 for Broken Rib.

4 Stripes

Working stripes can add a lot of color to a sweater. Each stripe can be the same number of rows or a random amount, using a total of two or more colors. Work in Stockinette Stitch (Option #1), working an even number of rows in each stripe. This allows the unused color to be carried loosely along the side edge of the piece. Twist the colors every 2 to 4 rows to prevent long strands along the edge.
(See examples on pages 49 and 73.)

What's Next?
Now that the Back is complete, choose one of four Front options.

CHAPTER THREE
Front Options
Pg. 91

Front Options

Decide whether you want to make a pullover or a cardigan, then choose either a crew neckline or a V-neckline. You can work in the same pattern stitch as the Back or choose something different.

CREWNECK PULLOVER

V-NECK PULLOVER

CREWNECK CARDIGAN

V-NECK CARDIGAN

Techniques used:
- K2 tog *(Fig. 7, page 124)*
- SSK *(Figs. 8a-c, page 124)*

1 Crewneck Pullover

(See examples on pages 37, 43, and 61.)

Work same as Back until Front measures approximately {8½-10-11½}{13-14½-16}"/ {21.5-25.5-29}{33-37-40.5} cm from bottom edge, ending by working a **wrong** side row: {51-55-59} {63-69-75} sts.

CREWNECK SHAPING

Both sides of Neck are worked at the same time using separate yarn for each side. Maintain established pattern throughout.

Row 1: Work across {20-21-22}{24-26-29} sts; with second yarn, work across center {11-13-15} {15-17-17} sts and slip these sts onto a st holder; work across: {20-21-22}{24-26-29} sts **each** side.

Rows 2-7: Work across first side; with second yarn, bind off 2 sts, work across: {14-15-16} {18-20-23} sts **each** side.

Work even until Front measures same as Back, ending by working a **wrong** side row; do **not** cut yarn.

With **right** sides together and Back in front of Front, work 3-needle bind off to join the left Front and Back shoulders *(Fig. 12, page 125)*.

Slip {14-15-16}{18-20-23} right shoulder sts from Back neck circular needle onto a straight needle, leaving remaining {23-25-27}{27-29-29} neck sts on circular needle. Using a double pointed needle, work 3-needle bind off to join the right Front and Back shoulders.

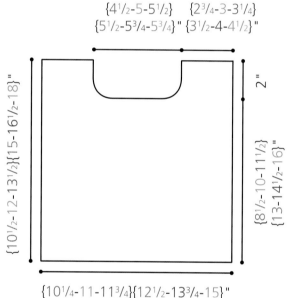

{4½-5-5½}   {2¾-3-3¼}
{5½-5¾-5¾}" {3½-4-4½}"

{10½-12-13½}{15-16½-18}"

2"

{8½-10-11½}
{13-14½-16}"

{10¼-11-11¾}{12½-13¾-15}"

2 V-Neck Pullover

(See examples on pages 19, and 31.)

Work same as Back until Front measures approximately {6-7-8}{9-10-11}"/{15-18-20.5} {23-25.5-28} cm from bottom edge, ending by working a **wrong** side row: {51-55-59} {63-69-75} sts.

Note: Place a marker around the first and last stitch to indicate Sleeve placement.

V-NECK SHAPING
Both sides of Neck are worked at the same time using separate yarn for each side. Maintain established pattern throughout.

Row 1: Work across {25-27-29}{31-34-37} sts, slip next st onto st holder for neck treatment; with second yarn, work across: {25-27-29}{31-34-37} sts **each** side.

Note: If working in Stockinette Stitch, the decreases can be worked one stitch in from the edge to make picking up stitches easier.

Sizes 6, 12, & 18 Months ONLY
Row 2: Work across; with second yarn, work across.

Row 3 (Decrease row): Work across to within 2 sts of neck edge, SSK; with second yarn, K2 tog, work across: {24-26-28} sts **each** side.

Repeat Rows 2 and 3, {10-11-12} times: {14-15-16} sts **each** side.

Sizes 2, 4, & 6 ONLY
Row 2: Work across; with second yarn, work across.

Row 3 (Decrease row): Work across to within 2 sts of neck edge, SSK; with second yarn, K2 tog, work across: {30-33-36} sts **each** side.

Rows 4-6: Work across; with second yarn, work across.

Row 7 (Decrease row): Work across to within 2 sts of neck edge, SSK; with second yarn, K2 tog, work across: {29-32-35} sts **each** side.

Repeat Rows 2-7, {5-6-6} times; then repeat Rows 2 and 3, {1-0-0} time(s) **more** *(see Zeros, page 121)*: {18-20-23} sts **each** side.

All Sizes
Work even until Front measures same as Back, ending by working a **wrong** side row; do **not** cut yarn.

With **right** sides together and Back in front of Front, work 3-needle bind off to join the left Front and Back shoulders *(Fig. 12, page 125)*.

Slip {14-15-16}{18-20-23} right shoulder sts from Back neck circular needle onto a straight needle, leaving remaining {23-25-27}{27-29-29} neck sts on circular needle. Using a double pointed needle, work 3-needle bind off to join the right Front and Back shoulders.

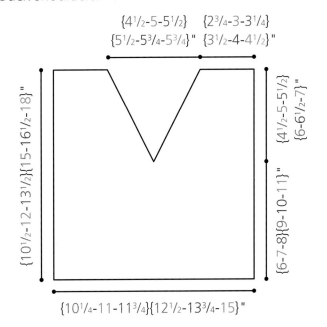

{4½-5-5½} {2¾-3-3¼}
{5½-5¾-5¾}" {3½-4-4½}"

{4½-5-5½}
{6-6½-7}"

{10½-12-13½}{15-16½-18}"

{6-7-8}{9-10-11}"

{10¼-11-11¾}{12½-13¾-15}"

3 Crewneck Cardigan

(See examples on pages 25, 55, and 73.)

LEFT FRONT
EDGING
Work one of the Edgings below to match the Back.

Garter Stitch, Ribbing, and Rolled Edge
Using straight needles, cast on {25-27-29}{31-35-37} sts.

Work same as Back *(Chapter 1, pages 86 & 87)*.

Picots
Using straight needles, place a slip knot on needle, add on 4 sts, bind off 2 sts in **knit**, slip st back onto left needle, ★ add on 5 sts, bind off 2 sts in **knit**, slip st back onto left needle; repeat from ★ until there are {24-27-27}{30-33-36} sts; add on {1-0-2} {1-2-1} st(s) *(see Zeros, page 121)*: {25-27-29} {31-35-37} sts.

Ruffle
Using straight needles, cast on {50-54-58} {62-70-74} sts.

Rows 1-12: Work same as Back *(Chapter 1, page 88)*: {25-27-29}{31-35-37} sts.

Lace
Work same as Back *(Chapter 1, page 88)* until Lace measures approximately {5-5¹/₂-5³/₄} {6¹/₄-7-7¹/₂}"/{12.5-14-14.5}{16-18-19} cm from cast on edge, ending by working Row 4.

Bind off first 3 sts in **knit** and remaining sts in **purl**.

With **right** side of Lace facing, pick up {25-27-29} {31-35-37} sts evenly spaced across straight edge.

BODY
Beginning with a **right** side row, work in same pattern as Back *(Chapter 2, page 90)* until Front measures approximately {6-7-8}{9-10-11}"/ {15-18-20.5}{23-25.5-28} cm from bottom edge.

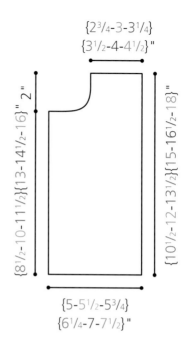

{2³/₄-3-3¹/₄}
{3¹/₂-4-4¹/₂}"

2"

{8¹/₂-10-11¹/₂}{13-14¹/₂-16}"

{10¹/₂-12-13¹/₂}{15-16¹/₂-18}"

{5-5¹/₂-5³/₄}
{6¹/₄-7-7¹/₂}"

Note: Place a marker around stitch at side edge to indicate Sleeve placement.

Work even until Front measures approximately {8¹/₂-10-11¹/₂}{13-14¹/₂-16}"/{21.5-25.5-29} {33-37-40.5} cm from bottom edge, ending by working a **right** side row.

CREWNECK SHAPING
Maintain established pattern throughout.

Row 1: Bind off {5-6-7}{7-9-8} sts, work across: {20-21-22}{24-26-29} sts.

Row 2: Work across.

Row 3 (Decrease row): Bind off 2 sts, work across: {18-19-20}{22-24-27} sts.

Rows 4-7: Repeat Rows 2 and 3 twice: {14-15-16} {18-20-23} sts.

Work even until Front measures same as Back, ending by working a **wrong** side row; do **not** cut yarn.

With **right** sides together and Back in front of Front, work 3-needle bind off to join the Left Front and Back shoulders *(Fig. 12, page 125)*

RIGHT FRONT

Work same as Left Front to Crewneck Shaping, ending by working a **wrong** side row; then work Crewneck Shaping same as Left Front.

Slip {14-15-16}{18-20-23} right shoulder sts from Back neck circular needle onto a straight needle, leaving remaining {23-25-27}{27-29-29} neck sts on circular needle. Using a double pointed needle, work 3-needle bind off to join the Right Front and Back shoulders.

4 V-Neck Cardigan

(See examples on pages 7, 13, 49, and 67.)

LEFT FRONT
EDGING
Work one of the Edgings below to match the Back.

Garter Stitch, Ribbing, and Rolled Edge
Using straight needles, cast on {25-27-29} {31-35-37} sts.

Work same as Back *(Chapter 1, pages 86 & 87).*

Picots
Using straight needles, place a slip knot on needle, add on 4 sts, bind off 2 sts in **knit**, slip st back onto left needle, ★ add on 5 sts, bind off 2 sts in **knit**, slip st back onto left needle; repeat from ★ until there are {24-27-27}{30-33-36} sts; add on {1-0-2} {1-2-1} st(s) *(see Zeros, page 121)*: {25-27-29} {31-35-37} sts.

Ruffle
Using straight needles, cast on {50-54-58} {62-70-74} sts.

Rows 1-12: Work same as Back *(chapter 1, page 88)*: {25-27-29}{31-35-37} sts.

Lace
Work same as Back *(chapter 1, page 88)* until Lace measures approximately {5-5½-5¾} {6¼-7-7½}"/{12.5-14-14.5}{16-18-19} cm from cast on edge, ending by working Row 4.

Bind off first 3 sts in **knit** and remaining sts in **purl**.

With **right** side of Lacing facing, pick up {25-27-29} {31-35-37} sts evenly spaced across straight edge.

BODY
Beginning with a **right** side row, work in same pattern as Back *(Chapter 2, page 90)* until Front measures approximately {6-7-8}{9-10-11}"/ {15-18-20.5}{23-25.5-28} cm from bottom edge, ending by working a **wrong** side row.

Note: Place a marker around the first and last stitch to indicate Sleeve and Neck Band placement.

V-NECK SHAPING
Maintain established pattern throughout.

Note: If working in Stockinette Stitch, the decreases can be worked one stitch in from the edge to make picking up stitches easier.

Sizes 6, 12, & 18 Months ONLY
Row 1 (Decrease row): Work across to last 2 sts, SSK: {24-26-28} sts.

Row 2: Work across.

Repeat Rows 1 and 2, {10-11-12} times: {14-15-16} sts.

Sizes 2, 4, & 6 ONLY
Row 1 (Decrease row): Work across to last 2 sts, SSK: {30-34-36} sts.

Row 2: Work across.

Row 3 (Decrease row): Work across to last 2 sts, SSK: {29-33-35} sts.

Rows 4-6: Work across.

Repeat Rows 1-6, {5-6-6} times; then repeat Row 1, {1-1-0} time(s) **more** *(see Zeros, page 121)*: {18-20-23} sts.

All Sizes
Work even until Front measures same as Back, ending by working a **wrong** side row; do **not** cut yarn.

With **right** sides together and Back in front of Front, work 3-needle bind off to join the Left Front and Back shoulders *(Fig. 12, page 125).*

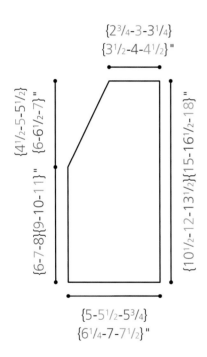

{2³/₄-3-3¹/₄}
{3¹/₂-4-4¹/₂}"

{4¹/₂-5-5¹/₂}"
{6-6¹/₂-7}"

{6-7-8}{9-10-11}"

{10¹/₂-12-13¹/₂}{15-16¹/₂-18}"

{5-5¹/₂-5³/₄}
{6¹/₄-7-7¹/₂}"

RIGHT FRONT
Work same as Left Front to V-Neck Shaping: {25-27-29}{31-35-37} sts.

Note: Place a marker around the first and last stitch to indicate Sleeve and Neck Band placement.

V-NECK SHAPING
Maintain established pattern throughout, working the placement of the decreases the same as the Left Front.

Sizes 6, 12, & 18 Months ONLY
Row 1 (Decrease row): K2 tog, work across: {24-26-28} sts.

Row 2: Work across.

Repeat Rows 1 and 2, {10-11-12} times: {14-15-16} sts.

Sizes 2, 4, & 6 ONLY
Row 1 (Decrease row): K2 tog, work across: {30-34-36} sts.

Row 2: Work across.

Row 3 (Decrease row): K2 tog, work across: {29-33-35} sts.

Rows 4-6: Work across.

Repeat Rows 1-6, {5-6-6} times; then repeat Row 1, {1-1-0} time(s) **more**: {18-20-23} sts.

All Sizes
Work even until Front measures same as Back, ending by working a **wrong** side row; do **not** cut yarn.

Slip {14-15-16}{18-20-23} right shoulder sts from Back neck circular needle onto a straight needle, leaving remaining {23-25-27}{27-29-29} neck sts on circular needle. Using a double pointed needle, work 3-needle bind off to join the Right Front and Back shoulders.

What's Next?
It's time to make the Sleeves, knitting them right onto the Body.

CHAPTER FOUR
Sleeve Options
Pg. 97

Sleeve Options

Sleeves are in four Body styles: cap, boxy, short, or long. Stitches for the Sleeves are picked up across the end of rows on the Front and Back, working between Back and Front markers. The Body of each Sleeve is then worked from the top down. Any Edging Option can be added.

CAP SLEEVE

BOXY SLEEVE

SHORT SLEEVE

LONG SLEEVE

Sleeve Body

Techniques used:
- K2 tog *(Fig. 7, page 124)*
- SSK *(Figs. 8a-c, page 124)*

1 Cap Sleeve

(See examples on pages 7 and 25.)

With **right** side of Body facing and using straight needles, pick up {45-51-55}{61-65-71} sts evenly spaced between markers *(Fig. 11a, page 125)*; remove markers.

Beginning with a **wrong** side row, work in same pattern as Back throughout.

Row 1: Work across in pattern.

Row 2 (Decrease row): K2 tog, work across to last 2 sts, SSK: {43-49-53}{59-63-69} sts.

Rows 3-7: Repeat Rows 1 and 2 twice, then repeat Row 1 once **more**: {39-45-49}{55-59-65} sts.

Work a Sleeve Edging, page 100, **or** bind off all sts in pattern.

Repeat for second Cap Sleeve.

2 Boxy Sleeve

(See examples on pages 37 and 55.)

With **right** side of Body facing and using straight needles, pick up {45-51-55}{61-65-71} sts evenly spaced between markers *(Fig. 11a, page 125)*; remove markers.

Beginning with a **wrong** side row, work in same pattern as Back until Sleeve measures approximately {4-5-6}{8-10-12}"/{10-12.5-15} {20.5-25.5-30.5} cm **or** to desired length to Edging, ending by working a **wrong** side row.

Work a Sleeve Edging, page 100, **or** bind off all sts in pattern.

Repeat for second Boxy Sleeve.

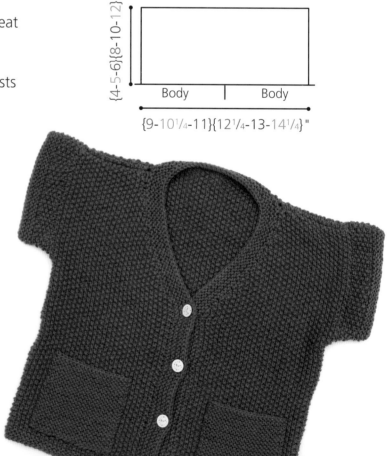

{4-5-6}{8-10-12}"

{9-10¼-11}{12¼-13-14¼}"

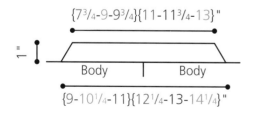

{7¾-9-9¾}{11-11¾-13}"

1"

{9-10¼-11}{12¼-13-14¼}"

3 Short Sleeve

(See examples on pages 13, 19, and 49.)

With **right** side of Body facing and using straight needles, pick up {45-51-55}{61-65-71} sts evenly spaced between markers *(Fig. 11a, page 125)*; remove markers.

Beginning with a **wrong** side row, work in same pattern as Back throughout.

Row 1: Work across in pattern.

Row 2 (Decrease row): K2 tog, work across to last 2 sts, SSK: {43-49-53}{59-63-69} sts.

Rows 3-10: Repeat Rows 1 and 2, 4 times: {35-41-45}{51-55-61} sts.

Work even until Sleeve measures approximately {2-2¹/₂-3}{3¹/₂-4-4¹/₂}"/{5-6.5-7.5}{9-10-11.5} cm, ending by working a **wrong** side row.

Work a Sleeve Edging, page 100, **or** bind off all sts in pattern.

Repeat for second Short Sleeve.

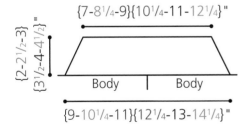

4 Long Sleeve

(See examples on pages 31, 43, 61, 67, and 73.)

With **right** side of Body facing and using straight needles, pick up {45-51-55}{61-65-71} sts evenly spaced between markers *(Fig. 11a, page 125)*; remove markers.

Beginning with a **wrong** side row, work in same pattern as Back throughout.

Rows 1-3: Work across in pattern.

Row 4 (Decrease row): K1, K2 tog, work across to last 3 sts, SSK, K1: {43-49-53}{59-63-69} sts.

Repeat Rows 1-4, {9-11-11}{13-14-16} times: {25-27-31}{33-35-37} sts.

Work even until Sleeve measures approximately {6-7-8}{10-12-14}"/{15-18-20.5}{25.5-30.5-35.5} cm **or** to desired length to Edging, ending by working a **wrong** side row.

Note: If you want to adjust the length of the Sleeve, just remember to allow for any length that the Edging adds. Generally with kids, it's safer to make the Sleeves too long and roll them up since they're growing all the time!

Work a Sleeve Edging, page 100, **or** bind off all sts in pattern.

Repeat for second Long Sleeve.

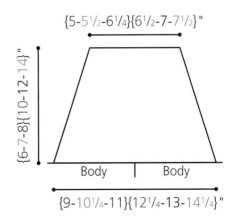

Sleeve Edging

Work any of the Edgings below to match the Back and Front, or work a different one if desired. When making Long Sleeves, be sure to bind off Sleeve Edging **loosely**.

Techniques used:
- YO and YO twice *(Figs. 3a & d, page 122)*
- Adding new stitches *(Figs. 4a & b, page 123)*
- Knit increase *(Figs. 6a & b, page 123)*
- P2 tog *(Fig. 10, page 124)*

GARTER STITCH
Knit 6 rows.

Bind off all sts in **knit**.

RIBBING
Row 1: K1, (P1, K1) across.

Row 2: P1, (K1, P1) across.

Rows 3-6: Repeat Rows 1 and 2 twice.

Bind off all sts in pattern.

ROLLED EDGE
Beginning with a **knit** row, work in Stockinette Stitch for 10 rows.

Bind off all sts in **knit**.

PICOTS
Bind Off Row: ★ Add on 2 sts, bind off 5 sts, slip st back onto left needle; repeat from ★ across until less than 6 sts remain, add on 2 sts, bind off remaining sts.

RUFFLES
Row 1: Knit increase in each st across doubling st count.

Beginning with a **purl** row, work 7 rows in Stockinette Stitch.

Knit 4 rows.

Bind off all sts in **knit**.

LACE
Bind off Sleeve sts.

Using straight needles, cast on 5 sts.

When instructed to slip a stitch, always slip as if to **purl**.

Row 1: WYIF slip 1, K2, YO twice, P2 tog: 6 sts.

Row 2 (Right side): YO, K2, P1, K3: 7 sts.

Row 3: WYIF slip 1, K2, P4.

Row 4: WYIB and slipping first st, bind off first 2 sts in **knit**, knit across: 5 sts.

Repeat Rows 1-4 until Lace measures same as bound off edge, ending by working Row 4.

Bind off first 3 sts in **knit** and remaining st in **purl**.

Sew straight edge of Lace to bound off edge of Sleeve.

What's Next?
Pockets - or just add an appliqué instead. If your sweater won't have either, you can begin the finishing steps.

CHAPTER FIVE

Pocket Options

Choose a pocket. Do you want a large or small pocket for the Front of the sweater? Or one to be placed inside of either a pullover or a cardigan and sewn to the Front and Back when sewing the side seams? Turn any crewneck sweater into a hoodie by adding a kangaroo pocket (pages 102 and 103) and a hood (pages 111 and 116).

PATCH POCKET

LARGE PULLOVER POCKET

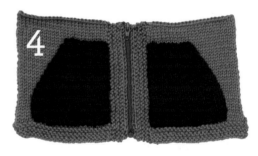

PULLOVER KANGAROO POCKET

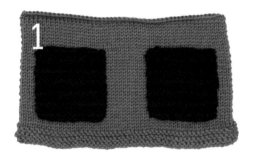

CARDIGAN KANGAROO POCKET

SIDE SEAM POCKET

Techniques used:
- K2 tog *(Fig. 7, page 124)*
- SSK *(Figs. 8a-c, page 124)*

1 Patch Pocket

A patch pocket can be added to a cardigan as well as a pullover. It can even be used as a breast pocket.
(See examples on page 7.)

Using straight needles, cast on {15-15-20}{20-20-20} sts.

Knit every row until Pocket measures approximately {3-3-4}{4-4-4}"/{7.5-7.5-10}{10-10-10} cm from cast on edge.

Bind off all sts in **knit** leaving a long end for sewing.

Using photo as a guide for placement, pin Pocket to Front, then sew in place.

2 Large Pullover Pocket

(See example on page 43.)

Using straight needles, cast on 30 sts.

Knit every row until Pocket measures approximately {3-3-4}{4-4-4}"/{7.5-7.5-10}{10-10-10} cm from cast on edge.

Bind off all sts in **knit** leaving a long end for sewing.

Using photo as a guide for placement, pin Pocket to Front, then sew in place.

3 Pullover Kangaroo Pocket

(See example on page 61.)

Using straight needles, cast on {41-41-41}{51-51-51} sts.

Beginning with a **purl** row, work in Stockinette Stitch for {1-1-1½}{2-2-2}"/{2.5-2.5-4}{5-5-5} cm, ending by working a **purl** row.

SHAPING
Row 1 (Decrease row): K5, K2 tog, knit across to last 7 sts, SSK, K5: {39-39-39}{49-49-49} sts.

Row 2: K5, purl across to last 5 sts, K5.

Repeat Rows 1 and 2, {9-9-9}{12-12-12} times: {21-21-21}{25-25-25} sts.

Bind off remaining sts in **knit** leaving a long end for sewing.

Using photo as a guide for placement, page 65, pin Pocket to Front, then sew in place along top, bottom, and straight side edges.

4 Cardigan Kangaroo Pocket

(See example on page 71.)

LEFT FRONT POCKET

Using straight needles, cast on {20-20-20} {25-25-25} sts.

Beginning with a **purl** row, work in Stockinette Stitch for {1-1-1½}{2-2-2}"/{2.5-2.5-4}{5-5-5} cm, ending by working a **purl** row.

SHAPING

Row 1 (Decrease row): K5, K2 tog, knit across: {19-19-19}{24-24-24} sts.

Row 2: Purl across to last 5 sts, K5.

Repeat Rows 1 and 2, {9-9-9}{12-12-12} times: {10-10-10}{12-12-12} sts.

Bind off remaining sts in **knit**.

Using photo as a guide for placement, pin Pocket to Left Front placing long vertical edge one stitch in from front edge, then sew in place along top, bottom, and straight side edges.

RIGHT FRONT POCKET

Using straight needles, cast on {20-20-20}{25-25-25} sts.

Beginning with a **purl** row, work in Stockinette Stitch for {1-1-1½}{2-2-2}"/ {2.5-2.5-4}{5-5-5} cm, ending by working a **purl** row.

SHAPING

Row 1 (Decrease row): Knit across to last 7 sts, SSK, K5: {19-19-19}{24-24-24} sts.

Row 2: K5, purl across.

Repeat Rows 1 and 2, {9-9-9}{12-12-12} times: {10-10-10}{12-12-12} sts.

Bind off remaining sts in **knit**.

Using Left Front as a guide for placement, pin Pocket to Right Front placing long vertical edge one stitch in from front edge, then sew in place along top, bottom, and straight side edges.

5 Side Seam Pocket (Make 2)

(See example on page 74.)

Using straight needles and leaving a long end for sewing, cast on {30-32-34}{36-38-40} sts.

Beginning with a **purl** row, work in Stockinette Stitch until Pocket measures approximately {3-3-3½}{3½-4-4}"/{7.5-7.5-9}{9-10-10} cm from cast on edge.

Bind off all sts leaving a long end for sewing.

Fold Pocket in half widthwise, with **right** side together. Sew across top and bottom edges.

Pin Pocket to **wrong** side of Front and Back placing bottom edge above the bottom Edging. Pocket will be sewn to the sweater when sewing side seams *(Chapter 7, page 110)*.

What's Next?
Add one of the cute appliqués or begin the finishing steps.

CHAPTER SIX

Appliqué Options

Appliqués personalize a sweater making it fun to wear. They can be sewn to a pocket or anywhere you please on the sweater.

SUN APPLIQUÉ

HEART APPLIQUÉ

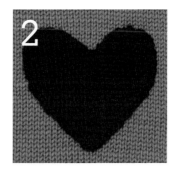

CAT APPLIQUÉ

STAR APPLIQUÉ

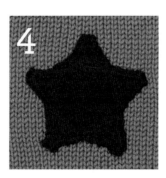

TRUCK APPLIQUÉ

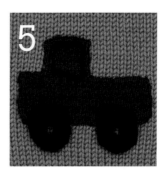

Techniques used:
- Adding new stitches (*Figs. 4a & b, page 123*)
- Knit increase (*Figs. 6a & b, page 123*)
- K2 tog (*Fig. 7, page 124*)
- SSK (*Figs. 8a-c, page 124*)
- P2 tog (*Fig. 10, page 124*)

1 Sun Appliqué

(See example on page 19.)

Using double pointed needles (*Figs. 2a & b, page 121*), cast on 8 sts.

Foundation Row: Purl across dividing sts onto 3 needles, arranged 3-3-2.

Begin working in rounds.

Rnd 1 (Right side): Knit increase in each st around; place marker around first stitch to indicate beginning of rnds (*see Markers, page 121*): 16 sts.

Rnds 2 and 3: Knit around.

Rnd 4: Knit increase in each st around: 32 sts.

Rnds 5-8: Knit around.

Rnd 9: ★ Add on 2 sts, bind off 5 sts in **knit**, slip st back onto left needle; repeat from ★ around to last 5 sts, add on 2 sts, bind off remaining sts leaving a long end for sewing.

Block appliqué so it lays flat (*see Blocking, page 126*).

Using photo as a guide, page 105, and Contrasting Color yarn or embroidery floss, embroider face using French knots for eyes and a backstitch mouth (*see Embroidery Stitches, page 126*).

Pin appliqué to sweater, then sew in place.

2 Heart Appliqué

(See example on page 55.)

Using straight needles, cast on 15 sts, place marker (*see Markers, page 121*), cast on 15 sts: 30 sts.

Row 1 (Right side): Knit increase, knit across to within 2 sts of marker, SSK, K2 tog, knit across to last st, knit increase.

Row 2: Knit across.

Rows 3-12: Repeat Rows 1 and 2, 5 times: 6 ridges.

Row 13 (Decrease row): Knit across to within 2 sts of marker, SSK, K2 tog, knit across: 28 sts.

Row 14: Knit across.

Rows 15 and 16: Repeat Rows 13 and 14: 26 sts.

Row 17 (Decrease row): SSK, knit across to within 2 sts of marker, SSK, K2 tog, knit across to last 2 sts, K2 tog: 22 sts.

Row 18: Knit across.

Rows 19 and 20: Repeat Rows 17 and 18: 18 sts.

Bind off remaining sts in **knit** leaving a long end for sewing.

Pin appliqué to sweater, then sew in place.

3 Cat Appliqué

(See example on page 37.)

Using straight needles, cast on 7 sts.

Row 1: Purl across.

Row 2 (Right side - Increase row): Knit increase, knit across to last st, knit increase: 9 sts.

Rows 3-8: Repeat Rows 1 and 2, 3 times: 15 sts.

Row 9: Purl across.

Row 10: Knit across.

Rows 11-15: Repeat Rows 9 and 10 twice, then repeat Row 9 once **more**.

FIRST EAR
Row 1: K6, leave remaining 9 sts unworked; **turn**.

Row 2: P2 tog, P4: 5 sts.

Row 3: K3, K2 tog: 4 sts.

Row 4: P2 tog, P2: 3 sts.

Row 5: K1, K2 tog: 2 sts.

Row 6: P2 tog; cut yarn and pull end through loop.

SECOND EAR
Row 1: With **right** side facing, bind off next 3 sts, knit across: 6 sts.

Row 2: P4, P2 tog: 5 sts.

Row 3: K2 tog, K3: 4 sts.

Row 4: P2, P2 tog: 3 sts.

Row 5: K2 tog, K1: 2 sts.

Row 6: P2 tog; cut yarn leaving a long end for sewing and pull end through loop.

Using photo as a guide, page 105, and Contrasting Color yarn or embroidery floss, embroider face using satin stitch for eyes and nose, and straight stitches for whiskers *(see Embroidery Stitches, page 126).*

Block appliqué so it lays flat *(see Blocking, page 126).*

Pin appliqué to sweater, then sew in place.

4 Star Appliqué

(See example on page 43.)

FIRST POINT
Using double pointed needles, place a slip knot on needle, add on 5 sts.

Points are worked in short rows using 2 needles. When instructed to slip a stitch, always slip as if to **purl** with yarn held to **wrong** side.

Row 1 (Right side): Knit across.

Row 2: P3, leave remaining 3 sts unworked; **turn**.

Row 3: Slip 1, K2.

Row 4: P5; **turn**.

Row 5: Slip 1, K4.

Row 6: P3; **turn**.

Row 7: Slip 1, K2.

Row 8: P6.

Row 9: Slipping first st, bind off all sts in **knit**; do **not** cut yarn: one st.

REMAINING 4 POINTS
Add on 5 sts: 6 sts.

Repeat Rows 1-9 of First Point.

CENTER
With **right** side of all Points facing, pick up 4 sts evenly spaced across straight edge of same Point and 5 sts evenly spaced along straight edge of remaining 4 Points *(Fig. 11a, page 125)*: 25 sts.

Divide sts onto 3 needles, arranged 8-8-9 *(Figs. 2a & b, page 121)*; place marker around first st to indicate beginning of rnd *(see Markers, page 121)*.

Rnd 1: Knit around.

Rnd 2: (SSK, K3) around: 20 sts.

Rnd 3: Knit around.

Rnd 4: (SSK, K2) around: 15 sts.

Rnd 5: Knit around.

Rnd 6: (SSK, K1) around: 10 sts.

Rnd 7: SSK around; cut yarn leaving a long end for sewing: 5 sts.

Thread yarn needle with end and slip remaining sts onto yarn needle; gather tightly to close center and secure end.

Block appliqué so it lays flat *(see Blocking, page 126)*.

Pin appliqué to sweater, then sew in place.

5 Truck Appliqué

Using straight needles, cast on 20 sts.

Rows 1-7: Beginning with a **purl** row, work in Stockinette Stitch (purl one row, knit one row).

Row 8: Bind off 9 sts in **knit**, knit across: 11 sts.

Row 9: Bind off 4 sts in **purl**, purl across: 7 sts.

Rows 10-15: Work in Stockinette Stitch for 6 rows.

Bind off all sts in **knit** leaving a long end for sewing.

TIRE (Make 2)
Using double pointed needles and Black, cast on 4 sts; ★ do **not** turn, slide sts to opposite end of needle, K4; repeat from ★ 12 times **more**.

Bind off all sts in **knit** leaving a long end for sewing.

Sew bound off sts to cast on sts.

Block appliqué so it lays flat *(see Blocking, page 126)*.

Using photo as a guide, page 105, and Black yarn or embroidery floss, embroider window with backstitch and headlight with a straight stitch *(see Embroidery Stitches, page 126)*.

Pin appliqué to sweater, then sew in place.

Sew Tires to Truck and sweater.

What's Next?
All that's left is the finishing: Sew the seams, add a neck treatment or a hood, then add a closure if desired and you're done!

CHAPTER SEVEN
Pullover Finishing
Options Pg. 109

CHAPTER EIGHT
Cardigan Finishing
Options Pg. 113

Pullover Finishing Options

Your sweater can have a Garter Stitch neck band, neck Ribbing, or a collar. Crewneck pullovers can also have a rolled neck edge or a hood.

This is a good time to sew the side and underarm seams. When you finish working the neckline treatment in this chapter, your sweater will be finished and ready to be worn and enjoyed!

CREWNECK OPTIONS

GARTER STITCH NECK BAND

NECK RIBBING

COLLAR

ROLLED NECK EDGE

HOOD

V-NECK OPTIONS

GARTER STITCH NECK BAND

NECK RIBBING

COLLAR

Seams

Seams: Unless Side Seam Pockets will be added, weave underarm and side in one continuous seam, one half stitch in *(Fig. 13, page 125)*.

Adding Side Seam Pockets: Beginning at bottom edge, weave side of Front and Back together along Edging, one half stitch in *(Fig. 13, page 125)*, then weave one side of Pocket in place. Weave remaining side of Pocket in place, then weave remaining side and underarm in one continuous seam.

Crewneck Options

1 Garter Stitch Neck Band

(See example on page 37.)

With **right** side facing, using double pointed needles *(Fig. 2b, page 121)* and placing approximately {18-19-21}{21-22-22} sts onto each of 3 needles, knit {23-25-27}{27-29-29} sts across Back neck circular needle, pick up 10 sts evenly spaced along left Front neck edge *(Fig. 11b, page 125)*, knit {11-13-15}{15-17-17} sts from Front neck st holder, pick up 10 sts evenly spaced along right Front neck edge; place marker around first st to indicate beginning of rnd: {54-58-62}{62-66-66} sts.

Rnd 1: Purl around.

Rnd 2: Knit around.

Rnds 3-8: Repeat Rnds 1 and 2, 3 times.

Bind off all sts **loosely** in **purl**.

2 Neck Ribbing

(See example on page 43.)

With **right** side facing, using double pointed needles *(Fig. 2b, page 121)* and placing approximately {18-19-21}{21-22-22} sts onto each of 3 needles, knit {23-25-27}{27-29-29} sts across Back neck circular needle, pick up 10 sts evenly spaced along left Front neck edge *(Fig. 11b, page 125)*, knit {11-13-15}{15-17-17} sts from Front neck st holder, pick up 10 sts evenly spaced along right Front neck edge; place marker around first st to indicate beginning of rnd: {54-58-62}{62-66-66} sts.

Rnds 1-5: (K1, P1) around.

Bind off all sts **loosely** in pattern.

3 Collar

Slip {6-7-8}{8-9-9} sts from Front neck st holder onto circular needle (holding Back neck sts), with **wrong** side facing, bind off one st in **knit**, knit across Front neck edge, pick up 10 sts evenly spaced along left Front neck edge *(Fig. 11b, page 125)*, knit {23-25-27}{27-29-29} sts across Back neck, pick up 10 sts evenly spaced along right Front neck edge, slip remaining {5-6-7}{7-8-8} sts from Front st holder onto left hand point of circular needle and knit across to bound off st; do **not** join: {53-57-61}{61-65-65} sts.

Knit every row for 3" (7.5 cm).

Bind off all sts **loosely** in **knit**.

4 Rolled Neck Edge

With **right** side facing, using double pointed needles *(Fig. 2b, page 121)* and placing approximately {18-19-21}{21-22-22} sts onto each of 3 needles, knit {23-25-27}{27-29-29} sts across Back neck circular needle, pick up 10 sts evenly spaced along left Front neck edge *(Fig. 11b, page 125)*, knit {11-13-15}{15-17-17} sts from Front neck st holder, pick up 10 sts evenly spaced along right Front neck edge; place marker around first st to indicate beginning of rnd: {54-58-62} {62-66-66} sts.

Knit 10 rounds.

Bind off all sts **loosely** in **knit**.

5 Hood

(See example on page 65.)

Technique used:
• M1 *(Figs. 5a & b, page 123)*

With **right** side facing, slip {5-6-7}{7-8-8} sts from Front neck st holder onto circular needle (holding Back neck sts), bind off next st (center), knit across remaining {4-5-6}{6-7-7} sts on st holder, pick up 10 sts evenly spaced along right Front neck edge *(Fig. 11b, page 125)*, knit {11-12-13}{13-14-14} sts across Back neck, place marker, knit across remaining {12-13-14}{14-15-15} Back neck sts, pick up 10 sts evenly spaced along left Front neck edge, knit across to bound off st: {53-57-61} {61-65-65} sts.

Row 1 (Wrong side): K5, purl across to last 5 sts, K5.

Row 2 (Increase row): Knit across to marker, M1, slip marker, K1, M1, knit across: {55-59-63} {63-67-67} sts.

Rows 3-20: Repeat Rows 1 and 2, 9 times: {73-77-81}{81-85-85} sts.

Work even until Hood measures approximately {8-8-8}{9-9-9}"/{20.5-20.5-20.5}{23-23-23} cm **or** to desired length.

Slide the sts to the center of the cable. Fold the cable in half with **right** sides together and pull it between the center sts forming a loop *(Fig. 1)*: {36-38-40}{40-42-42} sts on one side.

Work 3-needle bind off to join top of Hood, working last 3 sts together.

Fig. 1

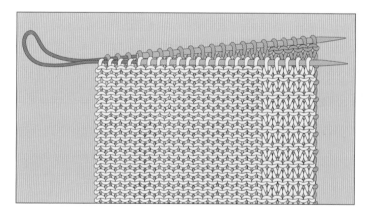

V-Neck Options

Technique used:
- Slip 2 tog as if to **knit**, K1, P2SSO *(Figs. 9a & b, page 124)*

1 Garter Stitch Neck Band

(See example on page 31.)

With **right** side facing, using double pointed needles *(Fig. 2b, page 121)* and placing approximately {23-25-27}{28-30-31} sts on each of 3 needles, knit {23-25-27}{27-29-29} sts across Back neck circular needle, pick up {22-24-26}{28-30-32} sts evenly spaced along left Front neck edge, slip center st from st holder onto empty needle and knit it, place marker around center st, pick up {22-24-26}{28-30-32} sts evenly spaced along right Front neck edge; place marker around first st to indicate beginning of rnd: {68-74-80}{84-90-94} sts.

Rnd 1: Purl across to marked st, K1, purl across.

Rnd 2 (Decrease rnd): Knit across to within one st of marked st, slip 2 tog as if to **knit**, K1, P2SSO, knit across: {66-72-78}{82-88-92} sts.

Rnds 3-6: Repeat Rnds 1 and 2 twice: {62-68-74}{78-84-88} sts.

Bind off remaining sts **loosely** in **purl**.

2 Neck Ribbing

With **right** side facing, using double pointed needles *(Fig. 2b, page 121)* and placing approximately {23-25-27}{28-30-31} sts on each of 3 needles, knit {23-25-27}{27-29-29} sts across Back neck circular needle, pick up {22-24-26}{28-30-32} sts evenly spaced along left Front neck edge, slip center st from st holder onto empty needle and knit it, place marker around center st, pick up {22-24-26}{28-30-32} sts evenly spaced along right Front neck edge; place marker around first st to indicate beginning of rnd: {68-74-80}{84-90-94} sts.

Rnd 1: (K1, P1) across to within one st of marked st, K3, P1, (K1, P1) across.

Rnd 2 (Decrease rnd): (K1, P1) across to within one st of marked st, slip 2 tog as if to **knit**, K1, P2SSO, P1, (K1, P1) across: {66-72-78}{82-88-92} sts.

Rnd 3: (K1, P1) around.

Rnd 4 (Decrease rnd): K1, (P1, K1) across to within one st of marked st, slip 2 tog as if to **knit**, K1, P2SSO, (K1, P1) across: {64-70-76}{80-86-90} sts.

Rnds 5 and 6: Repeat Rnds 1 and 2: {62-68-74}{78-84-88} sts.

Bind off all sts **loosely** in pattern.

3 Collar

(See example on page 19.)

With **wrong** side facing and using circular needle (holding Back neck sts), slip center st from Front st holder onto needle and purl it, pick up one st on Left Front neck edge, pass center st over the picked up st and off the needle, pick up {21-23-25}{27-29-31} sts evenly spaced along left Front neck edge, knit {23-25-27}{27-29-29} sts across Back neck, pick up {22-24-26}{28-30-32} sts evenly spaced along right Front neck edge; do **not** join: {67-73-79}{83-89-93} sts.

Knit every row for 3" (7.5 cm).

Bind off all sts **loosely** in **knit**.

Congratulations!
You customized a wonderful pullover. Are you ready to make another one?

Cardigan Finishing Options

Begin by sewing the seams. The Front Band and neckline treatment are worked separately on a crewneck and in one piece on a V-Neck. Choose between Garter Stitch and Ribbing; add a collar or a hood to a crew neckline. Work the closures, page 119, to complete your sweater.

CREWNECK OPTIONS
FRONT BAND AND NECKLINE TREATMENT

V-NECK OPTIONS

GARTER STITCH

RIBBING

COLLAR

HOOD

GARTER STITCH

RIBBING

Seams

Seams: Unless Side Seam Pockets will be added, weave underarm and side in one continuous seam, one half stitch in *(Fig. 13, page 125)*.

Adding Side Seam Pockets: Beginning at bottom edge, weave side of Front and Back together along Edging, one half stitch in *(Fig. 13, page 125)*, then weave one side of Pocket in place. Weave remaining side of Pocket in place, then weave remaining side and underarm in one continuous seam.

Crewneck Front Band Options

If using buttons for the closure, work the Buttonhole Band on the Right Front for a Girl's sweater and the Left Front for a Boy's sweater. Work the Plain Band on the remaining Front. If choosing any of the other closures, work the Plain Band on both Fronts.

Techniques used:
- YO *(Figs. 3a & c, page 122)*
- K2 tog *(Fig. 7, page 124)*

1 Garter Stitch

(See examples on pages 25, 55, and 73.)

BUTTONHOLE BAND
With **right** side facing and using straight needles, pick up {41-49-57}{65-71-79} sts evenly spaced along Front edge.

Rows 1-3: Knit across.

Place markers for buttonholes, placing a marker ³/₄" (2 cm) above bottom edge and ¹/₂" (1.25 cm) from top edge, then evenly spacing markers for remaining {2-2-3}{3-4-4} buttonholes.

Row 4 (Buttonhole row): ★ Knit across to marker, YO, K2 tog; repeat from ★ {3-3-4}{4-5-5} times **more**, knit across.

Rows 5-7: Knit across.

Bind off all sts **loosely** in **knit**.

PLAIN BAND
With **right** side facing and using straight needles, pick up {41-49-57}{65-71-79} sts evenly spaced along Front edge.

Knit 7 rows.

Bind off all sts in **knit**.

Work desired Crewneck Neckline treatment, pages 42 and 43.

2 Ribbing

BUTTONHOLE BAND
With **right** side facing and using straight needles, pick up {41-49-57}{65-71-79} sts evenly spaced along Front edge.

Row 1: K1, (P1, K1) across.

Row 2: P1, (K1, P1) across.

Row 3: K1, (P1, K1) across.

Place markers for buttonholes, placing a marker ¾" (2 cm) above bottom edge and ½" (1.5 cm) from top edge, then evenly spacing markers for remaining {2-2-3}{3-4-4} buttonholes.

Row 4 (Buttonhole row): ★ Work across in established pattern to marker, YO, K2 tog; repeat from ★ {3-3-4}{4-5-5} times **more**, work across.

Rows 5-7: Repeat Rows 1-3.

Bind off all sts in pattern.

PLAIN BAND
With **right** side facing and using straight needles, pick-up {41-49-57}{65-71-79} sts evenly spaced along Front edge.

Row 1: K1, (P1, K1) across.

Row 2: P1, (K1, P1) across.

Rows 3-7: Repeat Rows 1 and 2 twice, then repeat Row 1 once **more**.

Bind off all sts in pattern.

Work desired Crewneck Neckline treatment.

Crewneck Neckline Treatment

1 Garter Stitch Neck Band

(See examples on pages 25 and 73.)

With **right** side facing and using circular needle (holding Back neck sts), pick up 4 sts across Right Front Band and {5-6-7}{7-9-8} sts across bound off sts *(Fig. 11b, page 125)*, pick up 10 sts evenly spaced along neck edge, knit {23-25-27}{27-29-29} sts across Back neck, pick up 10 sts evenly spaced along Left Front neck edge, pick up {5-6-7}{7-9-8} sts across bound off sts and 4 sts across Front Band: {61-65-69}{69-75-73} sts.

Knit 5 rows.

Bind off all sts in **knit**.

Work desired Closure, page 119.

2 Neck Ribbing

With **right** side facing and using circular needle (holding Back neck sts), pick up 4 sts across Right Front Band and {5-6-7}{7-9-8} sts across bound off sts *(Fig. 11b, page 125)*, pick up 10 sts evenly spaced along neck edge, knit {23-25-27}{27-29-29} sts across Back neck, pick up 10 sts evenly spaced along Left Front neck edge, pick up {5-6-7}{7-9-8} sts across bound off sts and 4 sts across Front Band: {61-65-69}{69-75-73} sts.

Row 1: P1, (K1, P1) across.

Row 2: K1, (P1, K1) across.

Rows 3-6: Repeat Rows 1 and 2 twice.

Bind off all sts **loosely** in pattern.

Work desired Closure, page 119.

3 Collar

With **wrong** side facing and using circular needle (holding Back neck sts), skip Left Front Band and pick up {5-6-7}{7-9-8} sts across bound off sts *(Fig. 11b, page 125)*, pick up 10 sts evenly spaced along Left Front neck edge, knit {23-25-27}{27-29-29} sts across Back neck, pick up 10 sts evenly spaced along Right Front neck edge, pick up {5-6-7}{7-9-8} sts across bound off sts, leave Front Band unworked: {53-57-61}{61-67-65} sts.

Knit every row for 3" (7.5 cm).

Bind off all sts **loosely** in **knit**.

Work desired Closure, page 119.

4 Hood

(See example on page 56.)

Technique used:
• M1 *(Figs. 5a & b, page 123)*

With **right** side facing and using circular needle (holding Back neck sts), pick up 4 sts across Right Front Band and {5-6-7}{7-9-8} sts across bound off sts *(Fig. 11b, page 125)*, pick up 10 sts evenly spaced along neck edge, knit {11-12-13}{13-14-14} sts across Back neck, place marker, knit across remaining {12-13-14}{14-15-15} Back neck sts, pick up 10 sts evenly spaced along Left Front neck edge, pick up {5-6-7}{7-9-8} sts across bound off sts and 4 sts across Front Band: {61-65-69}{69-75-73} sts.

Row 1: K5, purl across to last 5 sts, K5.

Row 2 (Increase row): Knit across to marker, M1, slip marker, K1, M1, knit across: {63-67-71}{71-77-75} sts.

Rows 3-20: Repeat Rows 1 and 2, 9 times: {81-85-89}{89-95-93} sts.

Work even until Hood measures approximately {8-8-8}{9-9-9}"/{20.5-20.5-20.5}{23-23-23} cm **or** to desired length.

Slide the sts to the center of the cable. Fold the cable in half with **right** sides together and pull it between the center sts forming a loop *(Fig. 1, page 111)*: {40-42-44}{44-47-47} sts on one side.

Work 3-needle bind off to join top of Hood, working last 3 sts together.

Work desired Closure, page 119.

V-Neck Options

If using buttons for the closure, work the Buttonhole Band.
If choosing any of the other closures, work the Plain Band.

Techniques used:
- YO *(Figs. 3a & c, page 122)*
- K2 tog *(Fig. 7, page 124)*

1 Garter Stitch

(See examples on pages 13 and 118.)

BUTTONHOLE BAND

With **right** side facing, using circular needle (holding Back neck sts) and beginning at Right Front Edging, pick up {29-35-41}{47-53-55} sts evenly spaced across to marker, remove marker, pick up {22-24-26}{28-30-32} sts evenly spaced across neck edge to shoulder, knit {23-25-27}{27-29-29} sts across Back neck, pick up {22-24-26}{28-30-32} sts evenly spaced across Left Front neck edge to marker, remove marker for Girl's Buttonhole Band **only**, pick up {29-35-41}{47-53-55} sts evenly spaced across: {125-143-161}{177-195-203} sts.

Rows 1-3: Knit across.

Girl's Sweater Only - Row 4 (Buttonhole row): K3, YO, K2 tog, ★ K {10-8-10}{12-10-8}, YO, K2 tog; repeat from ★ {1-2-2}{2-3-4} time(s) **more**, knit across.

Boy's Sweater Only - Row 4 (Buttonhole row): Knit across to Left Front marker, YO, K2 tog, ★ K {10-8-10}{12-10-8}, YO, K2 tog; repeat from ★ {1-2-2}{2-3-4} time(s) **more**, K3.

Rows 5-7: Knit across.

Bind off all sts in **knit**.

Sew {3-4-4}{4-5-6} buttons to Front Band to correspond with buttonholes.

PLAIN BAND

With **right** side facing, using circular needle (holding Back neck sts) and beginning at Right Front Edging, pick up {29-35-41}{47-53-55} sts evenly spaced across to marker, remove marker, pick up {22-24-26}{28-30-32} sts evenly spaced across neck edge to shoulder, knit {23-25-27}{27-29-29} sts across Back neck, pick up {22-24-26}{28-30-32} sts evenly spaced across Left Front neck edge to marker, remove marker, pick up {29-35-41}{47-53-55} sts evenly spaced across: {125-143-161}{177-195-203} sts.

Knit 7 rows.

Bind off all sts in **knit**.

Work desired Closure, page 119.

2 Ribbing

(See examples on pages 49 and 67.)

BUTTONHOLE BAND

With **right** side facing, using circular needle (holding Back neck sts) and beginning at Right Front Edging, pick up {29-35-41}{47-53-55} sts evenly spaced across to marker, remove marker, pick up {22-24-26}{28-30-32} sts evenly spaced across neck edge to shoulder, knit {23-25-27}{27-29-29} sts across Back neck, pick up {22-24-26}{28-30-32} sts evenly spaced across Left Front neck edge to marker, remove marker for Girl's Buttonhole Band **only**, pick up {29-35-41}{47-53-55} sts evenly spaced across: {125-143-161}{177-195-203} sts.

Row 1: K1, (P1, K1) across.

Row 2: P1, (K1, P1) across.

Row 3: K1, (P1, K1) across.

Girl's Sweater Only - Row 4 (Buttonhole row): P1, K1, P1, YO, K2 tog, ★ work across {10-8-10} {12-10-8} sts in pattern, YO, K2 tog; repeat from ★ {1-2-2}{2-3-4} time(s) **more**, work across.

Boy's Sweater Only - Row 4 (Buttonhole row): Work across in pattern to Left Front marker, YO, K2 tog, ★ work across {10-8-10}{12-10-8} sts, YO, K2 tog; repeat from ★ {1-2-2}{2-3-4} time(s) **more**, work across.

Rows 5-7: Repeat Rows 1-3.

Bind off all sts in pattern.

Sew {3-4-4}{4-5-6} buttons to Front Band to correspond with buttonholes.

PLAIN BAND

With **right** side facing, using circular needle (holding Back neck sts) and beginning at Right Front Edging, pick up {29-35-41}{47-53-55} sts evenly spaced across to marker, remove marker, pick up {22-24-26}{28-30-32} sts evenly spaced across neck edge to shoulder, knit {23-25-27} {27-29-29} sts across Back neck, pick up {22-24-26} {28-30-32} sts evenly spaced across Left Front neck edge to marker, remove marker, pick up {29-35-41} {47-53-55} sts evenly spaced across: {125-143-161} {177-195-203} sts.

Row 1: K1, (P1, K1) across.

Row 2: P1, (K1, P1) across.

Rows 3-7: Repeat Rows 1 and 2 twice, then repeat Row 1 once **more**.

Bind off all sts in pattern.

Work desired Closure, page 119.

Closures

BUTTONS	SNAPS	ZIPPER	TIE
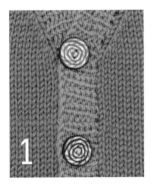	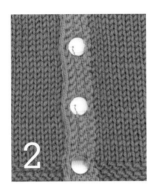		

1 Buttons

(See examples on pages 7 and 73.)

Sew buttons to Front Band to correspond with buttonholes.

2 Snaps

(See example on page 67.)

Block cardigan *(see Blocking, page 126)*.

Cut 2 pieces of grosgrain ribbon, each 1" (2.5 cm) longer than Front from bottom edge to neck shaping.
Fold ends under ½" (1.5 cm). Hand sew ribbon to **wrong** side of each Front along Front Band.

Attach snaps through knitting and ribbon, keeping in mind that a Girl's cardigan Front laps right over left and a Boy's cardigan laps left over right.

3 Zipper

(See examples on pages 55 and 118.)

Block cardigan *(see Blocking, page 126).*

Pin zipper in place carefully aligning bottom edge of zipper with edging of sweater. If zipper is too long for Front, open zipper, cut zipper length from the top, stitch a heavy zipper stop with thread and fold excess zipper to wrong side. Hand sew zipper in place.

4 Tie (Make 2)

(See examples on pages 13 and 25.)

Using double pointed needles, cast on 3 sts; ★ do **not** turn, slide sts to opposite end of needle, K3; repeat from ★ until Tie measures approximately 10" (25.5 cm) long.

Cut yarn; thread yarn needle with end and slip sts onto yarn needle; gather tightly to close and secure end; sew Tie to Crewneck Neck Band or bottom of V-Neck.

Congratulations!
*You customized a wonderful cardigan.
Are you ready to make another one?*

CHAPTER NINE

General Instructions

ABBREVIATIONS

cm	centimeters
K	knit
M1	make one
mm	millimeters
P	purl
pg.	page
P2SSO	pass 2 slipped stitches over
Rnd(s)	Round(s)
SSK	slip, slip, knit
st(s)	stitch(es)
tog	together
WYIB	with yarn in back
WYIF	with yarn in front
YO	yarn over

KNIT TERMINOLOGY

UNITED STATES	INTERNATIONAL
gauge =	tension
bind off =	cast off
yarn over (YO) =	yarn forward (yfwd) or yarn around needle (yrn)

SYMBOLS & TERMS

★ — work instructions following ★ as many **more** times as indicated in addition to the first time.

( ) or [ ] — contains explanatory remarks.

colon (:) — the number(s) given after a colon at the end of a row or round denote(s) the number of stitches you should have on that row or round.

work even — work without increasing or decreasing in the established pattern.

Yarn Weight Symbol & Names	LACE 0	SUPER FINE 1	FINE 2	LIGHT 3	MEDIUM 4	BULKY 5	SUPER BULKY 6
Type of Yarns in Category	Fingering, size 10 crochet thread	Sock, Fingering, Baby	Sport, Baby	DK, Light Worsted	Worsted, Afghan, Aran	Chunky, Craft, Rug	Bulky, Roving
Knit Gauge Range* in Stockinette St to 4" (10 cm)	33-40** sts	27-32 sts	23-26 sts	21-24 sts	16-20 sts	12-15 sts	6-11 sts
Advised Needle Size Range	000-1	1 to 3	3 to 5	5 to 7	7 to 9	9 to 11	11 and larger

*GUIDELINES ONLY: The chart above reflects the most commonly used gauges and needle sizes for specific yarn categories.

** Lace weight yarns are usually knitted on larger needles to create lacy openwork patterns. Accordingly, a gauge range is difficult to determine. Always follow the gauge stated in your pattern.

■□□□ BEGINNER	Projects for first-time knitters using basic knit and purl stitches. Minimal shaping.
■■□□ EASY	Projects using basic stitches, repetitive stitch patterns, simple color changes, and simple shaping and finishing.
■■■□ INTERMEDIATE	Projects with a variety of stitches, such as basic cables and lace, simple intarsia, double-pointed needles and knitting in the round needle techniques, mid-level shaping and finishing.
■■■■ EXPERIENCED	Projects using advanced techniques and stitches, such as short rows, fair isle, more intricate intarsia, cables, lace patterns, and numerous color changes.

KNITTING NEEDLES

U.S.	0	1	2	3	4	5	6	7	8	9	10	10½	11	13	15	17	19	35	50
U.K.	13	12	11	10	9	8	7	6	5	4	3	2	1	00	000	---	---	---	---
Metric - mm	2	2.25	2.75	3.25	3.5	3.75	4	4.5	5	5.5	6	6.5	8	9	10	12.75	15	19	25

GAUGE

Exact gauge is essential for proper fit. Before beginning your sweater, make a sample swatch in the yarn and needle specified in the individual instructions. After completing the swatch, measure it, counting your stitches and rows carefully. If your swatch is larger or smaller than specified, make another, changing needle size to get the correct gauge. **Keep trying until you find the size needles that will give you the specified gauge.**

ZEROS

To consolidate the length of a pattern, zeros are sometimes used so that all sizes can be combined. For example, cast on {0-1-2} sts, means the first size would do nothing, the second size would cast on one st, and the third size would cast on 2 sts.

MARKERS

As a convenience to you, we have used markers to indicate the beginning of a round, for placement of increases or decreases, or to mark the placement of Sleeves, Neck Band, and buttonholes.

Place markers as instructed. You may use purchased split ring or locked markers or tie a length of contrasting color yarn around the needle or a stitch.

When you reach a marker placed between stitches, slip it from the left needle to the right needle. When you reach a marker placed around a stitch, after working the stitch as indicated, move the marker up to the new stitch. Remove the marker(s) when no longer needed.

DOUBLE POINTED NEEDLES

The cast on stitches for the Sun appliqué are divided evenly between three double pointed needles *(Fig. 2a)*. Form a triangle with the needles. Make sure the cast on edge is not twisted.

When working too few stitches around a pullover neckline to use a circular needle, double pointed needles are required. Divide the stitches into thirds and slip one-third of the stitches onto each of 3 double pointed needles, forming a triangle.

With the fourth needle, work across the stitches on the first needle *(Fig. 2b)*. You will now have an empty needle with which to work the stitches from the next needle. Work the first stitch of each needle firmly to prevent gaps.

Fig. 2a

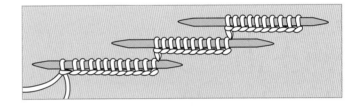

Fig. 2b

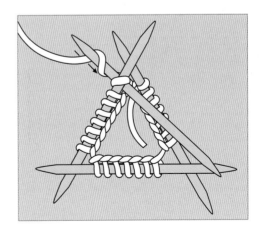

YARN OVER (abbreviated YO)

A yarn over is simply placing the yarn over the right needle creating an extra stitch. On the row following a yarn over, you must be careful to keep it on the needle and treat it as a stitch by knitting or purling it as instructed.

To make a yarn over, you'll loop the yarn over the needle like you would to knit or purl a stitch, bring it either to the front or the back of the piece so that it'll be ready to work the next stitch, creating a new stitch on the needle as follows:

After a knit stitch, before a knit stitch
Bring the yarn forward **between** the needles, then back **over** the top of the right hand needle, so that it is now in position to knit the next stitch (*Fig. 3a*).

Fig. 3a

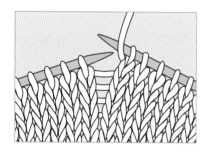

After a knit stitch, before a purl stitch.
Bring the yarn forward **between** the needles, then back **over** the top of the right hand needle and **forward** between the needles again, so that it is now in position to purl the next stitch (*Fig. 3b*).

Fig. 3b

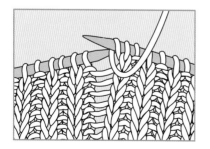

After a purl stitch, before a knit stitch
Take the yarn **over** the right hand needle to the back, so that it is now in position to knit the next stitch (*Fig. 3c*).

Fig. 3c

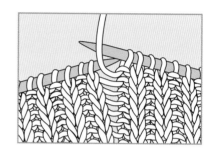

Yarn over twice
★ Bring the yarn forward **between** the needles, then back **over** the top of the right hand needle; repeat from ★ once **more**, then bring the yarn **forward** between the needles again, so that it is now in position to purl the next stitch (*Fig. 3d*).

Fig. 3d

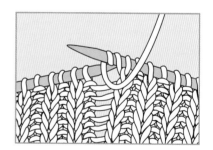

ADDING NEW STITCHES

Insert the right needle into the stitch as if to **knit**, yarn over and pull the loop through *(Fig. 4a)*. Insert the left needle into the loop just worked from **front** to **back** and slip the loop onto the left needle *(Fig. 4b)*. Repeat for the required number of stitches.

Fig. 4a

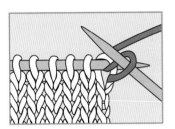

Fig. 4b

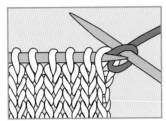

MAKE ONE *(abbreviated M1)*

Insert the left needle under the horizontal strand between the stitches from the **front** *(Fig. 5a)*, then **knit** into the **back** of the strand *(Fig. 5b)*.

Fig. 5a

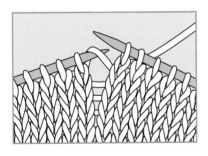

Fig. 5b

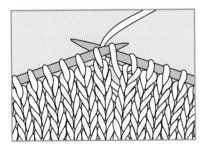

KNIT INCREASE

Knit the next stitch but do **not** slip the old stitch off the left needle *(Fig. 6a)*. Insert the right needle into the **back** loop of the **same** stitch and knit it *(Fig. 6b)*, then slip the old stitch off the left needle.

Fig. 6a

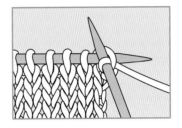

Fig. 6b

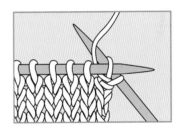

KNIT 2 TOGETHER
(abbreviated K2 tog)

Insert the right needle into the **front** of the first two stitches on the left needle as if to **knit** *(Fig. 7)*, then **knit** them together as if they were one stitch.

Fig. 7

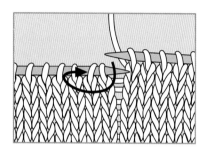

SLIP, SLIP, KNIT *(abbreviated SSK)*

Separately slip two stitches as if to **knit** *(Fig. 8a)*. Insert the left needle into the **front** of both slipped stitches *(Fig. 8b)* and then **knit** them together as if they were one stitch *(Fig. 8c)*.

Fig. 8a   Fig. 8b

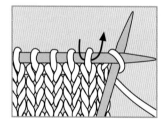   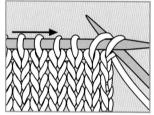

Fig. 8c

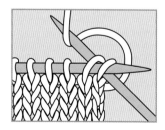

SLIP 2 TOGETHER, KNIT 1, PASS 2 SLIPPED STITCHES OVER
(abbreviated slip 2 tog as if to knit, K1, P2SSO)

With yarn in back, slip two stitches together as if to **knit** *(Fig. 9a)*, then knit the next stitch. With the left needle, bring both slipped stitches over the knit stitch *(Fig. 9b)* and off the needle.

Fig. 9a

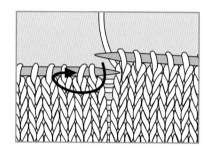

Fig. 9b

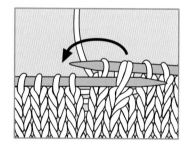

PURL 2 TOGETHER
(abbreviated P2 tog)

Insert the right needle into the front of the first two stitches on the left needle as if to **purl** *(Fig. 10)*, then purl them together as if they were one stitch.

Fig. 10

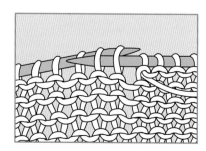

PICKING UP STITCHES

When instructed to pick up stitches, insert the needle from the **front** to the **back** under two strands at the edge of the worked piece *(Figs. 11a & b)*. Put the yarn around the needle as if to **knit**, then bring the needle with the yarn back through the stitch to the right side, resulting in a stitch on the needle.

Repeat this along the edge, picking up the required number of stitches. A crochet hook may be helpful to pull yarn through.

Fig. 11a

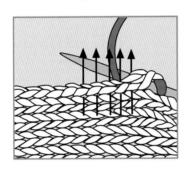

Fig. 11b

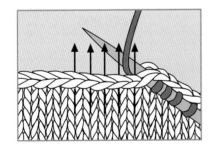

3-NEEDLE BIND OFF

With **right** sides together and needles parallel to each other, insert a third needle as if to **knit** into the first stitch on the front needle **and** into the first stitch on the back needle. Knit these two stitches together *(Fig. 12)* and slip them off the needles.
★ Knit the next stitch on each needle together and slip them off the needles. To bind off, insert one of the left needles into the first stitch on the right needle and bring the first stitch over the second stitch and off the right needle; repeat from ★ across until all of the stitches on the Front shoulder or Hood have been bound off; cut yarn and pull end through loop.

Fig. 12

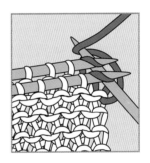

WEAVING SEAMS

The seams are sewn one half stitch in. With the **right** sides together and edges even, sew through both sides once to secure the beginning of the seam. Inserting the needle from **front** to **back**, catch **one** strand from each edge *(Fig. 13)*. Inserting the needle from **back** to **front** on the next row, catch one strand from each edge. Continue in this manner, being careful to match rows.

Fig. 13

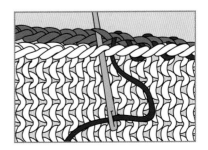

BLOCKING

Check the yarn label for any special instructions about blocking. Place your project on a clean terry towel over a flat surface and shape it to size. Place a damp cloth on top and hold a hand held steamer or steam iron just above the item and steam it thoroughly. Never let the weight of the iron touch the item because it will flatten the stitches. Allow the item to dry flat, away from heat or sunlight.

EMBROIDERY STITCHES
FRENCH KNOT

Bring the needle up at 1. Wrap the yarn around the needle the desired number of times and insert the needle at 2, holding the end of the yarn with non-stitching fingers *(Fig. 14)*. Tighten the knot, then pull the needle through, holding the yarn until it must be released.

Fig. 14

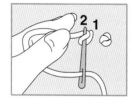

BACKSTITCH

The backstitch is worked from right to left. Come up at 1, go down at 2 and come up at 3 *(Fig. 15)*. The second stitch is made by going down at 1 and coming up at 4.

Fig. 15

STRAIGHT STITCH

Straight stitch is just what the name implies, a single, straight stitch. Come up at 1 and go down at 2 *(Fig. 16)*.

Fig. 16

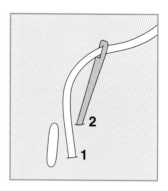

SATIN STITCH

Satin stitch is a series of straight stitches worked side by side so they touch but do not overlap *(Fig. 17a)* **or** come out of and go into the same stitch *(Fig. 17b)*. Come up at odd numbers and go down at even numbers.

Fig. 17a   Fig. 17b

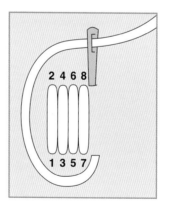 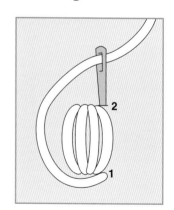

Yarn Information

The sweaters in this leaflet were made using medium weight yarn. Any brand of medium weight yarn may be used. It is best to refer to the yardage/meters when determining how many skeins or balls to purchase. Remember, to arrive at the finished size, it is the GAUGE/TENSION that is important, not the brand of yarn.

For your convenience, listed below are the yarns used to create our photography models.

BUTTONED V-NECK CARDIGAN
Lion Brand® *Cotton-Ease*®
#191 Violet

SHORT SLEEVE TOPPER
Universal Yarn *Cotton Supreme*
#605 Phlox

SUNSHINE PULLOVER WITH COLLAR
Universal Yarn *Cotton Supreme*
Main Color - #512 Hot Pink
Contrasting Color - #520 Yellow

RUFFLED TOPPER
Lion Brand® *Cotton-Ease*®
Main Color - #195 Azalea
Contrasting Color - #103 Blossom

V-NECK PULLOVER WITH POCKETS
Brown Sheep *Cotton Fleece*
CW310 Wild Orange

LACE TOP WITH A CAT
Universal Yarn *Classic Worsted*
Main Color - #618 Red
Contrasting Color - #651 White
Black #650

STAR POCKET PULLOVER
Red Heart® *Soft*® Yarn
Main Color - #4412 Grass Green
Contrasting Color - #4600 White

ZIPPERED STRIPED CARDI
Stitch Nation by Debbie Stoller™ *Bamboo Ewe*™
Main Color - #5875 Twilight
Contrasting Color - #5910 Lipstick

ZIPPERED HEART HOODIE
Caron® *Simply Soft*® Brites
Main Color - #9604 Watermelon
Contrasting Color - #9601 Coconut

HOODED SWEAT SHIRT
Cascade Yarns *22 0 Superwash*®
#812 Turquoise

SNAPPED V-NECK CARDI
Cascade Yarns *220 Superwash*®
#814 Hyacinth

STRIPED CREWNECK CARDI
Caron® *Simply Soft*® Brites
Main Color - #9610 Grape
Contrasting Color - #9607 Limelight

Project Journal

This page can be used to keep a record of the sweaters you create.

Recipient _____

Date _____

Size _____

Yarn _____

Color _____

Edging _____

Fabric _____

Front Style _____

Sleeve Style _____

Pocket(s) _____

Appliqué _____

Neckline _____

Closure _____

Recipient _____

Date _____

Size _____

Yarn _____

Color _____

Edging _____

Fabric _____

Front Style _____

Sleeve Style _____

Pocket(s) _____

Appliqué _____

Neckline _____

Closure _____

To: _____

From: _____

Date: _____

CARE INSTRUCTIONS

_____

_____

_____

_____

_____